THE
LOST
BOY

THE LOST BOY

TALES OF A CHILD SOLDIER

AYIK CHUT DENG

with CRAIG HENDERSON

VINTAGE BOOKS
Australia

VINTAGE

UK | USA | Canada | Ireland | Australia
India | New Zealand | South Africa | China

Vintage is part of the Penguin Random House group of companies whose addresses
can be found at global.penguinrandomhouse.com

First published by Vintage in 2020

Cover photographs © Emily Darling (portrait of the author);
Andrew Holt/Alamy Stock Photo
Cover design by Adam Laszczuk © Penguin Random House Australia Pty Ltd
Typeset in 12/18 pt Sabon by Midland Typesetters, Australia
Printed and bound in Australia by Griffin Press, part of Ovato, an accredited
ISO AS/NZS 14001 Environmental Management Systems printer

A catalogue record for this
book is available from the
National Library of Australia

ISBN 978 0 14379 629 9

penguin.com.au

For my family

CONTENTS

FOREWORD

If you are born in Australia then you've won life's lottery.

It's a simplistic, almost self-serving cliché, I know. But in essence, it's true. I am not suggesting that this wide brown land is the only 'Lucky Country' on earth (mind you, along with New Zealand, it's pretty hard to beat). I am not denying that many Aussies have to struggle and scrape by in order to succeed. Not everybody makes it. But in general, the healthcare, education and social justice systems in Australia will at least give you a chance at life – a fair go.

By contrast, you could have been born in the dust of war-torn Sudan in the late 1970s. Out there, where you have 'no dreams or ambitions, beyond the next five minutes', survival is your simple goal in life. The odds of tribal warfare or an encounter with an AK-47 are stacked heavily against that.

This is Ayik Chut Deng's truly remarkable survival story. At times it's a colourful and almost amusing tale – in a bizarre, unbelievable way – but ultimately it's a searing saga that left me shaking my head in amazement. I thought I'd read more than I needed to know about Sudanese boy soldiers, who, as Ayik recounts, 'had grown used to death, but never numbed by it.' I hadn't. Ayik was a tribal Dinka boy whose wonderful mum worshipped puff adders until she found her Christian God. Now an impressive, handsome man in his early forties, Ayik's been an Australian citizen for almost half his life, although how he survived his more recent 'lost years' on Queensland's Gold Coast is another miracle.

I first met Ayik in 2017 when I was hosting an SBS primetime series called *Look Me in the Eye*. An intelligent reality program (I know that sounds slightly ridiculous), the premise of the show was to bring together two implacably estranged people to see if by looking into each other's eyes for a few minutes without talking, they might come to some kind of reconciliation, maybe even find a little peace at last.

Ayik and his Sudanese childhood torturer and sworn mortal enemy, Anyang, confronted each other after decades of hatred and anger before our TV cameras in the show's very first episode. They each thought the other was long dead, until their eyes met across a crowded church in suburban Brisbane. It was compelling television – as powerful as any I have witnessed. As tears rolled down their cheeks, they finally embraced and Anyang begged forgiveness.

Ayik is an intrinsically decent yet understandably damaged man. It's clear he is recovering from what we now recognise as a genuine war disability: post-traumatic stress disorder (PTSD). Now, having a sense of how incessantly violent, painful and emotionally scarring Ayik's childhood must have been, I am pleased to have played even a small part in his reconciliation and the start of his long-term recovery. I am honoured to call Ayik a friend, happy to listen or offer a shoulder to lean on occasionally. *The Lost Boy* puts life's trials and tribulations into perspective. It's a riveting read.

Ray Martin
December 2019

PROLOGUE

I screamed like a baby but no more tears would come; I had already cried them all. The taste of soil was in my mouth as Anyang and his lieutenants rained more blows down on me. They had tied me like a captured animal: arms yanked behind my back with a rope cinched tight around my elbows and lashed to my bound ankles. The arrangement was so extreme I worried my shoulder bones might crack or my arms might be pulled from their sockets. As I lay facedown in the dirt under the African sun, my skin sloughed off like wet paper where the coarse rope sawed through it. At that moment there was nothing in my world other than total, endless, blinding pain.

Anyang wasn't done with me yet, though. He used to take the suffering up a notch or two by rubbing chilli powder into the welts and cuts he'd inflicted. Sometimes the pain would cause me to pass out. Other times I'd search his face for some sign of compassion but there was nothing – just a mask of brutality. It's hard to believe we were just kids; Anyang was sixteen and I was small, skinny and barely thirteen years old.

My sin – the reason for the torture – had been to escape from the army training camp I'd ended up in after the war began. Tens of thousands of Sudanese boys like Anyang and me fed the ranks of the Red Army – a ragtag force of killer kids who were being primed to lay down our lives in the fight for an independent South Sudan. We hailed from ethnic tribal groups throughout the south: ancient homelands that were under threat from Arab-controlled government forces in the north. As the uneducated sons of humble cattlemen, though, we had to be schooled in the art of war.

For eight months we were instructed on how to set ambushes, conduct patrols, carry out assaults, set up camps, dig foxholes, handle guns and munitions, form defensive positions and – above all – take orders. In the beginning I was as eager as the next boy to fight, but mainly because it meant I would get my own AK-47 assault rifle like the ones I'd seen young men carrying as the war edged closer to my village.

If I had a gun of my own I could not only shoot Arabs but also avenge the death of my big brother, who'd been murdered in the civil war. After two months of training, however, I wanted nothing more to do with the Red Army or killing, so I ran away, only to be caught and brought back to face the wrath of my teenage tormentor, Anyang.

Each time it was the same. Captured boys would be twisted and tied into the excruciating backwards knot, then the whipping would begin. Anyang's relative seniority among recruits, who ranged in age from ten to twenty, saw him placed in charge of discipline – a job he executed with focus and vigour. He beat us and whenever he got too sweaty or tired he ordered other boys to flay us with heavy, pliable wet roots from a tree that grew out of the river. Twenty lashes. Thirty lashes. Fifty lashes. Enough so our tears would run out.

Afterwards we were thrown into a bush prison built from thorny branches, where we lay pathetically in the dirt like discarded scraps. When the sun was highest in the sky we were pulled out of the cage and forced to sink into the nearby river. The relief was fleeting; we were extracted and ordered to lie down and roll on the hot ground, thirty metres one way then thirty metres back again, over and over until our tattered clothes were dry.

Next we had to squat and hop like rabbits for an hour and then run to the point of exhaustion. Finally, when we were on the brink of emotional and physical collapse, Anyang forced us to stand on one leg. If the other leg touched the ground, he would scream at us and have us flayed some more. If his subordinates didn't whip us hard enough, Anyang would snatch their canes from them and beat them until they hurt us to his satisfaction.

The physical recovery from this 'discipline' could take days, even weeks. The mental recovery? It could very well take a lifetime. But I would soon be so desperate to escape the Red Army that I would run away again, and again, and again.

A lot of young boys died in that frightful camp. I helped carry their withered corpses away and I dug their little graves, too, although hyenas sometimes exhumed and ate the dead. I don't know how or why I survived, although I did ask God every day to not only spare me but – when the time came for deployment – to assign me to the same unit as Anyang.

I daydreamed about how I was going to slowly put an end to that boy. At first, I planned, there would be a lot of pain for him. As my Red Army training drew to an end, though, I settled on an orderly, straight-up execution instead. As soon as I found myself alone with Anyang, I intended to raise the barrel of my Kalashnikov to his head, look him in the eye and pull the trigger.

It never happened. Anyang and I were swept along different paths during the war. Years passed, and I figured he was dead – killed in action like so many thousands of Sudan's boy soldiers. It seemed God had a different plan for me – one that would take me halfway around the world to begin a new life in Australia.

The Lucky Country would give me a second chance and the opportunity to mend my war-blackened heart and soul. Murder and revenge, it seemed, were not written into the script. I guess that's why they say the Lord moves in mysterious ways. Still, I never in a million lifetimes expected God would bring me face to face with Anyang again. When He did, many years later and in a suburban Brisbane church of all places, I knew exactly what to do: I would have to kill him and suffer the consequences, no doubt spending the rest of my days in a Queensland prison yard. It seemed such a pointless way for it all to end. I hoped God had other ideas instead.

1

A DIFFERENT WORLD

'When you were a baby you were dropped on your head,' my darling mum will sometimes remind me. 'You landed on a brick.'

I'm told that accidental tumble from the arms of my eldest sister Aguil left me with a depressed fracture of the skull – right in the middle of my forehead. It also left Mum in no doubt that this was the reason I was 'different' from other children in our tribe.

Unlike my brothers and sisters, and just about every other kid in our village, I was fascinated by things most people considered dangerous. As a boy I loved to play with scorpions; the bigger they were, the better. As soon as I'd catch one I'd secretly cut the venomous stinger from the tip of its tail and terrorise other children – either chasing them with the disarmed bug or throwing it onto their heads. It was such a great game.

I had no fear of snakes either and I could often be found bustling about in the endless grasslands of southern Sudan trying to catch them or generally harassing them with sticks. Bullies didn't scare me and I would always step in forcefully whenever I thought someone weaker was being pushed around. My mum said I was a cheeky, quick-tempered and fearless little boy. All the kids in the village saw it a different way. 'Oh, that guy is crazy.'

As I grew a bit older, though, something came to our village that scared me as much as it did all the other people in my tribe. A war. Over time, the conflict would teach me that some bullies have guns, grenades, tanks and jet bombers. I would discover that bullets are more lethal than any snakebite and no matter how fearless or different your mamma says you are, when bombs start raining down you run for your life just like everybody else.

The country of my birth, the East African nation of Sudan, had already been ravaged by a civil war that raged between 1955 and 1972. That was all before my time, though, and I was lucky to be born during a brief stretch of uneasy peace sometime around 1977. Although my early childhood memories were spared the horrors of conflict, Sudan's truce would prove to be short-lived. My battles awaited me but in the meantime I would have to face many other hardships, each one worse than being dropped on my head.

—

Just like me, my dad had a childhood fascination with snakes, a character trait that would alter the path of his life. His name was Chut Deng Achouth, and he was born into the Ayual clan of the Dinka people in a place called Wangulei, a village in the Twic region of southern Sudan. On top of being the largest ethnic group in southern Sudan, the Dinka have the distinction of being the tallest humans in Africa, and some are said to be owners of the blackest skin, too. My dad was no exception; as a boy I marvelled at the gigantic man who stood at the head of our family.

In spite of our towering presence, the Dinka have traditionally lived modest, uncomplicated and gentle lives in perfect harmony with nature. For many centuries we have raised cattle, farmed crops and sung our songs in simple grass-hut villages along the fertile plains and swamplands that flank the White Nile as it whispers north towards the Sahara Desert and Egypt. The enormous artery of the river pulses through the heart of our existence, as it sustains the long-horned cows and bulls we dedicate our lives to raising and protecting.

Dinka must have a million songs that tell of our love for the majestic animals we call weng and the blessings they bring us: milk, status, joy and – on sacred occasions like weddings and in sacrifice to the gods – meat. In a commodity-free society, a herd of cattle is the Dinka's truest measure of wealth.

It was this beautiful, bucolic future that beckoned my father until the day he decided it would be a good idea to mess with an angry cobra.

Dad was around fourteen and apparently out taking care of cattle in the fields when he glimpsed the familiar twist of a serpent in the bush. True to form, he went after it but instead of him triumphantly digging the cobra from a hole in the dirt, the thing rounded on him and spat a stream of venom into his eye. By the next day Dad couldn't see properly out of his poisoned pupil and it only got worse.

Since there were no doctors in the village, Dad's parents sold some cows to pay for him to get hospital treatment at a place called Mading Bor. But by the time Dad finally arrived it was too late; he never saw out of that eye again.

After this brush with modern medicine, Dad could have simply returned to his tribal life among the cows and the crops but, despite being half-blind, he glimpsed a different future for himself: one brimming with possibilities more dazzling than the acquisition of cattle, wives and grass huts. Instead of heading home he travelled to Khartoum – the sprawling, low-built capital of Sudan nearly a thousand kilometres away in the arid north of the country.

Because northern Sudan – a largely desert region – had long been governed by Arabs, Islam had been practised there for centuries. In the lush, arable south, however, Dinka clans worshipped animals as gods and also gave praise to a supreme creator called Nhialic – the god of the sky and the rain. Some Dinka even prayed to a deity called Jesus, the one the travelling white missionaries talked about. In time I would do so myself, but in my father's clan, God was a Nile eagle.

Back then, only Muslims were permitted to attend school in the north, and Dad apparently had no problem turning his back on the eagle and converting to Islam. Suitably pious, he attended classes and studied medical sciences. Dad became what would probably be considered a nurse or a paramedic in the West and helped tend to patients in a government hospital in Khartoum. This made him an important man, particularly back in the tribe, where a formal education – let alone a profession – was practically unheard of. Everybody called my father 'Dr Chut'.

In keeping with his new religion, Dad married an Arab-Muslim woman. They had children and settled into family life in a run-down rented dwelling outside Khartoum. Although life in the big city seemed to suit him, Dad couldn't ignore the strong pull of his tribal roots, which required him, as a proud Dinka man, to take a Dinka wife. Since Dinka men can marry as many women as they please – especially if they have a lot of cows to fatten their dowries – all Dad had to do was return to the tribal lands in the south to find a bride.

My mother, Achol Aguin Majok, was a shy and humble girl from the Dinka Twic ethnic group. As a member of the Awulian clan she worshipped the deadly puff adder and made daily offerings of oil to honour it. She was given to Dr Chut and after they wed in a tribal ceremony, he took her back to Khartoum to live.

Mum was uneducated and couldn't speak a word of Arabic, the universal language of Sudan, so she stayed home to cook and clean. Eventually Mum provided Dad with seven more kids: I arrived right in the middle of the brood, sandwiched between my big brother Aleer and older sisters Aguil and Yar, and my little brothers, Deng and Garang and, finally, my baby sister Akeer.

We didn't stay in Khartoum long enough for many clear memories to remain with me. When I was old enough to walk and talk, Dad was transferred to a new job in Juba, a much smaller town that served as the quasi capital of the less developed but infinitely more beautiful southern Sudan. Juba is where Garang and Akeer were born. His role at the local hospital may have earned Dad some respect but his higher station in life didn't translate into any great wealth. We were all crammed into a rented semi-permanent one-room hut. While our parents provided enough food to feed us, it often felt like there was only just enough to go around.

By the age of four or five I often found myself at the local garbage dump, scavenging for food with a friend or two. It might sound depressing and disgusting but those forays into other people's filth brought moments of modest culinary awakening. The first time I tasted Coca-Cola, for instance, was via the dregs in a grime-covered bottle salvaged from a pile of trash in Juba. For a boy who was used to just milk and water it tasted like liquid sunshine.

More often than not we'd find bread or bits of fruit and vegetables that richer families had thrown out. We also discovered that clambering through mounds of rubbish could be as dangerous as it was nourishing. On one occasion I gashed my left calf on a broken bottle so badly that the huge flap of skin dangling off it had to be sewn back on – African-style, with no anaesthetic and me screaming as I wrapped my bony arms around my eyes.

Sometimes more than just household waste would make its way to the dump. One day a friend and I came upon what at first looked like a rolled-up bag or blanket but, when I took a look inside, proved to be a man. He was sort of flat and he smelled awful. I didn't really know what to make of him at the time – after all, I was no older than five. When I look back today I feel desperately sorry for the soul who'd been so poorly regarded that someone likely murdered him and put him out with the garbage.

The dump encounter wasn't the first time I'd seen a dead body, either. One of my earliest memories is being at a Sunday market not far from our home. It was crowded with people selling food and wares when a commotion erupted: a fight between Mandari tribesmen and a rival ethnic group. People dived for cover and I ran as fast as I could. A moment later I saw a huge man with black cere-monial bands wrapped around his biceps lying motionless on his back in middle of the market. The smooth shaft of an arrow pointed skywards from his chest as if he'd been pinned to the earth like a bug on a table. I scurried away and hid. Later on, I found out the bow and arrow is the weapon of choice among the Mandari.

About a year later, I saw death rear its head yet again. This time it was much closer to home. As a public servant, Dad had only been assigned to the hospital in Juba for a fixed term and when he was told he would have to transfer to another far-flung town, he point-blank refused to leave. That apparently caused a problem. The man who was supposed to take over his role, a guy who was from the Kakwa tribal group, was none too pleased. He wanted that job badly, but Dad dug in. They argued angrily. The Kakwa man finally left, but not before warning Dad, 'I'll make sure only one of us has this job.'

A few days later the Kakwa man returned. Things appeared to have cooled and he offered Dad a cup of tea during a work break. His own cup just happened to spill onto the floor. Not long after drinking the tea, Dad started vomiting and having seizures. A doctor gave him some medication and told him to go home until he got better. Dad did as he was told, but back at home he blacked out in his chair and never regained consciousness.

Although there was no autopsy or toxicology report, there was a strong suspicion that Dad had been poisoned. One of my uncles who helped bury him said that in death my dad's skin had turned a lurid shade of purple. Later on, I found out poison is a Kakwa weapon of choice. Whatever the cause of death, my father was gone forever.

The year was 1983 and it was to be a turning point for me. Not only was it the year I was robbed of my dad at the age of six, it also heralded the start of the Second Sudanese Civil War – the catastrophic conflict that would ultimately reshape my country and, in the process, dramatically and permanently alter the lives of millions of South Sudanese people like me. Millions more would die.

As they buried my dad in Juba, however, to me there was

still the illusion of peace in the south. Besides, ?
else big was about to happen to me – the start (
Dinka life. As a widow with hungry children to care 101,
Mum had no choice but to return to Awulian, the village of
her mother in the Twic region, about three hundred kilometres north of Juba. There, her relatives gave her some
cows and land to farm, and almost overnight my chaotic
years in the dangerous ramshackle cities came to an end
and my life as a tribal Dinka boy burst into bloom. Instead
of scaling rubbish heaps I stood naked on the earth and
gazed across the lush, empty grasslands in the golden haze
of an African sunset. Although I had lost my father, for the
first time in my life I felt happy and content. I was where
I was always supposed to be. I had no idea a terrible storm
was gathering just over the horizon.

—

'Ahhh!' The little boy yelped in fright and ran straight into
his aunty's arms, leaving me standing alone with a stinger-
less scorpion in my hand and laughing at my practical joke.

Yes, life in Awulian was very good. Generally speaking,
in Dinka culture the maternal side of the family treats
children much more gently than the father's side, whose
job it is to toughen kids up. And so it was for me. Without
my big brother Aleer and eldest sister Aguil, who'd stayed
in the city to study, in Twic my mum and grandma, Duop,
took care of the rest of us. A host of loving uncles and
aunties helped them, happy to show us the tribal ways.

It turned out I wasn't the only Dinka who liked to play practical jokes. When we first arrived, my newfound relatives offered me a meal of awala-wala – a millet-flour staple of the Dinka diet – in a hollowed-out gourd that served as a bowl. I hungrily gobbled a few mouthfuls using my fingers before suddenly dropping it and reeling away in disgust. The thin layer of awala-wala had been carefully arranged to disguise the bowl's true contents: a pile of fresh cow shit.

'Welcome to the village, little town boy!' my relatives howled as they rolled about laughing.

That didn't stop me from slipping comfortably into tribal life. Compared to the city, the Dinka world was very beautiful and completely fulfilling, and it suited an energetic young boy like me perfectly. People worked hard in the tribe – we needed to, in order to survive in a subsistence economy. On top of caring for the cattle herds the tribe had to weed and tend to their crops: mostly sorghum and a little maize. There was hunting and cooking to be done, cows to be milked and huts to be built and maintained, including luaks – massive grass domes used to house our cattle at night when the herds weren't grazing further afield.

Most projects were communal and everyone pitched in if someone needed help. Dinka commerce was a system of barter. There was no money, no shops, no running water, no machines and no electricity. We didn't even have clothes. Save for some ceremonial beads and a few skimpy adornments, our lives were lived entirely naked.

In the drier months, when the rainfall slowed and grass for the cattle grew sparse around the village, the men gathered their herds and made a several-weeks-long journey to fertile grazing land along the White Nile. Boys were allowed to go along and I always went with my uncles. It was a time I loved more than anything. We'd be gone for a month or so, caring for maybe one thousand head of cattle at a time, and we survived by hunting for deer, antelope, giraffes, rabbits, lizards, elephants and tiang, or fishing and spearing pythons in the mighty Nile. I loved it and I felt safe, most of the time.

Everything is hungry in Sudan so we had to take precautions against wild animals and stay on the lookout for danger. All the children were taught to gather together each day just before sunset to go into the bush to have a shit – whether you had to go or not. This was to ensure no one was dragged away by a pack of hyenas. After a while, relieving myself at sunset became a habit.

Us kids also had a very important job in the tribe. Every morning we would help collect all the cow shit, break it down and spread it on the ground to dry out under the sun. In the late afternoon the dried dung would be gathered into big piles and set alight, sending up plumes of sweet-smelling smoke that settled over the camp like a huge misty blanket, helping keep the mosquitos at bay. The next day we'd rub the powdery, peach-coloured ash from the burned shit onto our skin as an insect repellent, sun-block and natural antiseptic – an all-in-one treatment that had served the Dinka well for centuries.

I learned that cow piss was very useful, too, but more for reasons of fashion than practicality. Somewhere along the line some smart cookie had discovered the ammonia in cow urine could bleach our black hair and turn it a fetching shade of orange-red. First you collect cow dung, burn it, then make a paste with ash and the cow urine and then wear it on your hair for a day. Then, after you wash the paste off, you put your head under the pissing cow and chemistry will gradually do the rest. After a week or so of repeating the treatment in our great outdoor salon, we'd be rewarded with funky red hair that was perpetually on-trend in Dinka culture. The women loved it.

Soon enough the rains would start again and we'd walk the herds back to the village on higher ground. The cattle always came first; everything we did and everywhere we went was about their wellbeing. We'd cover them in dung ash, polish their horns and adorn them with trinkets and tassels made of dried-out cows' tails. If we were grazing by the Nile we'd tie them to the ground at night. If we were in the village, we'd herd them into a luak for safekeeping. The women and girls would milk them.

Being Dinka was a lot of work but that's not to say there was no time for play. If I wasn't harassing snakes and scorpions I was chasing and playing with my siblings, cousins and other children. Sometimes we'd start up a Dinka version of 'cops and robbers' using harmless homemade spears and pretend guns in mock battles. On other days our game of choice was a tribal take on 'mummies and daddies'. Fashioning little cattle herds out of clay, we'd arrange them in a make-believe village we scratched out in the dirt. We'd pretend to be married and the girls would harvest imaginary crops and cook while us boys discussed farming and looked after the pint-sized pottery cows.

Female Dinka didn't go hunting but as a young boy I was allowed to tag along with the older guys. I could usually be found scuttling around at their feet – especially if they managed to spear something big like an antelope. Since large kills were brought back and divided up to be shared among the different families, I'd make sure I was front and centre so I could be the one to take the meaty spoils assigned to the Chut family back to our home. My motivation wasn't greed, pride or impatience – I did it simply because I was devoted to my mum.

After my father was killed I felt a strong urge to look after Mum as best I could. I was forever bringing her little treasures – cowhides to use as sleeping mats and pieces of animals to put in the family pot. In return, Mum was always patient with me – maybe she was forever mindful of my head-first encounter with the brick back in Khartoum. She even sort of excused me the time I deliberately killed her god. I'd managed to corner a puff adder one day and for some reason I felt it necessary to burn it alive using sticks from the fire. Although I was punished, the penalty was light compared to what Dad would have dealt out, although he had himself been a renowned harasser of snakes.

Beyond raising cattle and having wives, there were two pastimes the men in our village aspired to in order to make their mark. One was wrestling and the other was singing. I had my heart set on becoming a singer.

Songs are the history books of Dinka culture; they are how we chart our journeys, how we pass on knowledge, worship the gods, celebrate our victories, mourn lost loved ones, warn of dangers, diss each other, introduce ourselves and declare our love for each other and the wonders of the world. We make up songs about anything that is worthy of attention or celebration. In my case, I really only wanted to sing songs about my beloved bull calf.

When my big sister Aguil was brought back to the village for her arranged marriage, our family received cows in exchange for her. One of the cows gave birth to a bull and that bull was given to me. He was my dearest possession and I fussed over him like he was a god. He was a beautiful animal, blessed with black-and-white markings and perfect white lips. Everybody knew how much I loved that bull so I was given the nickname Makerdit, which roughly translates to 'Bull the great'. I wasted little time writing love songs about him. I can't remember all the words but one verse stands out:

I will polish his horns with dung ash,
His horns will shine bright in the sun,
Just like my girlfriend's teeth . . .

Only I didn't have a girlfriend – I was too young for anything like that. But I did have that little bull and he meant the world to me. He also broke my heart. One day when we took the herd out to graze in the bush, my bull somehow wandered off and became stuck fast between two tree trunks. Normally hyenas would kill an animal trapped like that but when I found my beautiful pride and joy in the morning he didn't have a mark on him. He was dead all the same. I fell into a grief deeper than any pain I had ever felt before – even after losing my father. When Dad died I cried because Mum was crying; I think I was too young to properly process the enormity of that loss. Yet my sorrow at losing that baby bull would pale alongside the emotional torment I would soon have to face.

It wasn't unheard of for strangers to come into the tribal lands, and foreigners could readily be found in the cities. I was four or five when I first saw a white person. Mum and I were out in the street in Juba when a little boy with a mop of blond hair came and stood next to me, accompanied by his parents. When he put his arm next to mine I couldn't quite believe what I was seeing. The contrast between black and white skin was mind-blowing to me and I had no idea what to make of it. Speechlessly, I looked up at Mum in the hope she might be able to explain.

'It's all right,' she soothed. 'They're from a different world.'

Strangely, I obsessed over the boy's white skin. I was jealous of it and liked it far better than my own. Secretly I wished I could be a white person one day, too. There was something clean and magical about pale skin and light-blue and -brown eyes that intrigued me. A couple of years later I started to see a few more white people about the place. Two of them even came through our village on motorbikes, most likely adventurous tourists from the West. Some of the younger kids in the tribe were terrified by the sudden appearance of strange-looking white men riding noisy contraptions, but not me. After all, I knew they were just creatures from a different world – nothing to be frightened of. The bikers managed to explain that they wanted to get their hands on some salt and cooking oil. Being the crazy one in our village, I volunteered to be their guide.

Before I knew it I was perched stark naked on the back of a motorbike and hurtling along a dirt track faster than I thought it was possible for a human to move. We even outran the rain that had been falling in the village. I held onto the white man for dear life and managed to direct him to the neighbouring village of another Dinka clan, about a twenty-minute ride away.

A market was on when we arrived and as the bikers bartered for some oil and salt, all the little kids gathered around the bikes to stare at me. I knew right away what they were thinking: Who is this little black kid with the white men? And what is he doing on that motorbike? I couldn't help but feel that my pillion passenger heroics in the village that day would have provided good material for a song but I never went back to find out if anyone had written one.

When the bikers returned me to my own village they gave me a bag containing some fine brown powder and gestured that it was something I could eat. I tentatively put a bit on my tongue and was almost bowled over by the burst of warm sweetness that erupted in my mouth. I don't get quite that excited about it nowadays but any time I make a glass of Milo I remember that rainy day when I first tasted it – and the white bikers who brought it to me from a different world.

Not every visitor to our village came in search of adventure, oil and salt, though. Some came for blood.

2

NORTH AND SOUTH

'Quickly! Quickly! Come!' I could see Mum was frightened and that terrified me. She frantically gathered us kids together and we stumbled hurriedly away from the village. Like Mum, I'd also heard the blowing of a distant horn a few moments earlier but I only vaguely knew what it meant; apparently it was some kind of warning. But the look in Mum's eyes and the sight of men urgently grabbing spears made it clear: we were about to be attacked.

'Shhh!' Mum urged as we ran as far away as we could get. 'If they find you,' she panted, 'they will take you.'

For centuries the Dinka had shared southern Sudan's sweeping savannahs with other ethnic groups. Some of them were bitter rivals, most notably the Murle people and the Nuer, who make up the second-largest group behind Dinka. There are many other groups right across Sudan, too – Kakwa, Madi, Toposa, Mandari, Didinga and so on – about sixty in total. But it was the Nuer and the Murle the Dinka feared the most.

Those people thought nothing of raiding our villages to steal cattle and abduct children. In Mum's family alone, six people had been murdered by the Murle and seventeen kids had been kidnapped to be brainwashed, branded with that tribe's markings and raised as someone else's child. On this day, though, the horn warned us of Murle raiders. No wonder Mum was so scared.

I never saw what happened in the village, thanks to Mum's pre-emptive evacuation, but when it was all over one of our men lay dead from spear wounds. Some cattle had been stolen, too, but all of the children were safe.

It was common for skirmishes like that to result in relatively low casualties, mostly because traditional spears required close-range contact to inflict real damage. But times were changing in our part of the world. Before too long, the lethality of the weapons – and the scale of the body count – exploded.

Ethnic tribal tensions weren't the only political problems plaguing Sudan when I was a boy. There was a simmering, unresolved animosity between the lighter-skinned Arabs in the north and the black natives in the south. Like all of history's worst feuds, this one had deep, twisted roots.

It's thought ancient herders began farming and fishing along the Nile as far back as 7000BC. Kingdoms and cultures rose and fell through the millennia as great tides of people washed across the African continent, including, at some point, the Dinka.

During the rise of the Ottoman Empire around five hundred years ago, the northern part of what became known as Sudan was slowly but surely overtaken by Arabic culture as Muslim rule fanned out from Turkey. The very name 'Sudan' comes from early Turkish travellers, who referred to the lower reaches of the eastern Sahara Desert and the lush swamplands and savannahs to the south as Bilad-al-sudan. Translated into English, this bluntly means 'land of blacks'.

In the south – where my forebears worshipped snakes, eagles and the god of the sky and the rain – Islam showed no sign of taking hold. Christian missionaries, however, spread news of the gospel and turned more and more southerners to Christ.

Thankfully the Arabs kept mostly to the desert-blanketed north, which flourished as an economic centre and a hub for the slave trade due to Khartoum's location at the meeting point of the White Nile and the Blue Nile. Even when a brutal Islamic regime led by a hardline Messianic priest named Muhammad Ahmad overthrew the capital in 1881 and declared Sharia law throughout all Sudan, Ahmad and his followers (called the Mahdists) still couldn't exert meaningful control over people in the south.

The Mahdist reign was short-lived. In 1899 the British, who at the time occupied neighbouring Egypt, invaded alongside Egyptian soldiers, defeating the Mahdist forces and establishing a protectorate in Sudan. This Anglo-Egyptian rule led to a period of relative stability that lasted more than half a century.

The Brits could see Sudan wasn't a single, unified country but rather two separate nations: the south was populated almost exclusively by black tribal groups who were either animist, Christian or something in between, while the north was overwhelmingly Arabic in culture and Islamic in religion. Although Khartoum remained the capital, under the Brits the two territories were governed as separate regions.

In 1946, however, having barely consulted with southern leaders, Britain merged the two Sudans into one administrative domain. This sudden reversal of policy allowed the Arabs to concentrate power in the north. They assumed an exclusionary stance towards people in the south, in spite of their demands for proper representation and a measure of autonomy. A decade later, the Brits walked away from the colonisation of North Africa altogether and handed control over all of Sudan to the Arab government in Khartoum.

Although this newly minted Sudan gained independence on 1 January 1956, the first shots in what would become known as the First Sudanese Civil War had already been fired. In 1955, army bases in the south rose in mutiny after Khartoum looked like backing away from commitments to grant self-rule to the south when the new government was constituted. Although the uprisings failed, the surviving mutineers fled into the bush, where they morphed into a poorly armed, poorly equipped and poorly organised insurgency.

Over the next few years the haphazard rebels operated as little more than an ineffective and disparate clutch of guerrilla forces from various tribal groups. Attempts to unite were hamstrung by age-old tribal distrust and divisions. Meanwhile, the northern government was having its own problems with factionalism and disunity. This instability on both sides meant the war sputtered along with no real progress until the mid-1960s, when the divergent fighters from Dinka, Nuer, Madi, Lotuko, Bari and other southern ethnic groups were finally organised under a central command. This new separatist force called itself the Anyanya guerrilla army – anyanya being the Madi word for 'snake venom'.

The ensuing period of the war was known as the Anyanya Rebellion, a vicious campaign that would claim hundreds of thousands of lives. As the newly energised black southern separatists became more effective against the Muslim-controlled government army, they gained the support of northern Sudan's other enemies, predominantly the neighbouring nation of Ethiopia, which happened to be mostly Christian. The fighting resulted in the death of half a million people – most of them civilians – and the displacement of many more until a peace agreement was reached between Anyanya and Khartoum in the Ethiopian capital of Addis Ababa in 1972.

In exchange for an end to hostilities, southern Sudan was to be ruled as a single administrative region and southerners were also granted limited powers of autonomy. But even before the ink was dry, former Anyanya commanders scoffed that the deal was too flimsy to prop up any kind of lasting peace. They were proven to be dead right.

Believing the full independence of southern Sudan was the only way to guarantee peace, some ex-Anyanya commanders maintained rebel forces during the 1970s and early 1980s as they waited for the inevitable breakdown of relations with the north.

Meanwhile, many other former Anyanya fighters had been absorbed into the Sudanese Army, headquartered in Khartoum. One such commander was Dr John Garang – a Dinka man who would become known as a founding father of South Sudanese independence.

Up in the north, a powerful rump of Muslim fundamentalists were also furious about the 1972 Addis Ababa Agreement and its concessions to southern self-rule. Things came to a head politically during the early 1980s when the increasingly hardline government in Khartoum eventually tore up the agreement, declared all of Sudan an Islamic state and, ultimately, pushed for the nationwide introduction of strict and brutal Sharia law.

This terrifying development stirred the dormant rebel forces in the south and also alarmed Dr John Garang, who was by then a colonel in the Sudanese Army. In 1983, Khartoum sent Dr Garang to his home territory of Bor, not too far from my village, to help quell a garrison of southern soldiers who were on the verge of mutiny. Instead of stopping them, Dr Garang helped them pull it off. They killed the northern soldiers in Bor and Dr Garang took the mutineers into the bush where they re-organised themselves into what became known as the Sudanese People's Liberation Army, or SPLA.

As a united rebel force, the SPLA not only had the tentative support of many southern Sudanese in the 'land of blacks', it ultimately earned the backing of neighbouring countries, particularly Ethiopia, Kenya and Uganda. It was the beginning of the catastrophe that came to be called the Second Sudanese Civil War. This conflict would be different from the first one; it would endure for longer, it would cost many more lives, it would eventually lead to an independent South Sudan . . . and I would have to play a part in it.

—

The first time I saw an AK-47 assault rifle I just knew I had to have one. It was 1984 and the gun in question was cradled in the wiry arms of a young soldier who'd arrived in our village. Months earlier, strange mobs of people had started flooding through Twic on foot in ever-increasing numbers. They couldn't speak Dinka and I couldn't understand a word they were saying, either. These travellers would stay overnight before leaving in the morning, always heading east.

'There is a war coming so these people are going to Ethiopia,' one of the tribal elders explained to me. 'Some are going there to be safe from the fighting, but the men are going to Ethiopia to get trained so they can come back and fight the Arab raiders.'

As usual, Mum had read the danger signs long before I knew anything was wrong. Over the previous months she'd noticed a slow, steady exodus of young men from the villages. These guys were meant to be the protectors of the community, the teachers and providers who guided the little ones, so when they all left to join the SPLA, Mum's heart filled with dread. When her oldest son – my big brother, Aleer – answered the rebel call too, the war really started to crash in on our family.

By 1984 the SPLA was going to villages throughout the south to tell the tribal chiefs that men in their late teens and twenties were needed as recruits. It wasn't a blanket edict or outright conscription – if a family had only one son he wouldn't be required to join, he could stay in the village and help care for his loved ones. But if a family had three or four sons? The oldest would be told to serve in the SPLA. Like a lot of the early rebel soldiers, however, my brother Aleer didn't need to be asked to fight for South Sudanese freedom – he eagerly volunteered.

Aleer had remained in Juba to study at university after our father died and the day he suddenly appeared in the village was one of the happiest of my short life. I'd been jumping up and down with excitement at seeing him, only to feel shattered a few days later when he joined a caravan of young men heading east towards an uncertain future. I watched Aleer leave, walking further and further away across the baking hot ground until shimmering wisps of heat mirage wrapped around him and pulled him from view. I was so heartbroken to lose Aleer again that I wept for two days straight. I didn't know it was the last time I would ever see him.

Many months later, word reached us that Aleer had been

killed before he even made it to the SPLA training base in Ethiopia. Witnesses relayed the story to our elders. Because Aleer was an educated man, he had been placed in a leadership position even before he underwent formal training. As his group of recruits embarked on the months-long walk from Twic to the border with Ethiopia, Aleer and a couple of others were handed AK-47s and ammunition and told, 'You're in charge. You're responsible for the rest of these people.'

Late one night as the group was travelling through a tribal area, one of the other temporary leaders got drunk and started firing rounds into the air.

'Stop it!' Aleer told him. 'There are people sleeping here, children sleeping. These are our people!'

But apparently the drunk guy couldn't help himself, perhaps also drunk on the power an assault rifle brings. He resumed his midnight machine-gunning so Aleer snatched the weapon from him. 'You don't listen, man,' he told the rogue. 'I'm keeping your gun until we get where we're going or until you can stop behaving like an idiot.'

After travelling for a few more hours, Aleer felt the troublemaker had sobered up and calmed down so he handed the gun back. The group continued walking but the guy just re-loaded the AK-47 and shot Aleer in the back of the head.

Today I find it hard to visualise Aleer's face and when I do think of him it is as a small, blurred shape on a far and dusty horizon. The bitter memory always makes me cry.

Before too long, more and more freshly trained soldiers returned from Ethiopia and travelled through my village.

As ever, I was fascinated by the young men in the uniforms and their stylish weapons of wood and iron. I also burned to avenge Aleer and that would require a gun, but with no way of getting one I had to make do by fashioning my own mock rifles out of clay.

Although my tribal life as a budding cattleman continued, I spent more and more time hanging around the soldiers whenever they were in the village, helping them out, cleaning their guns and generally getting in the way. To me, the rebels represented my lost brother and I was in awe of the bravery and pride they showed in standing up to the Islamists from the north. By this time, Mum no longer worshipped the puff adder; she had heard the teachings of the gospel and had given herself to Christ. Since I tended to follow my mum's lead in all important matters, I considered myself a Christian from that point onwards, too. All the more reason, I thought then, to hate the Arabs.

Sometimes our village would give the soldiers a cow or a bull to slaughter for food and, as usual, I was always on hand to help them skin it. They usually let me have some cow guts or the bloodied hide, and now and then they'd cut a hoof off the beast and toss it to me: 'Here you go, little man. Take this home.' I'd run straight to Mum and give her the spoils for her cooking pot.

As more soldiers came to our village, the more we heard the sound of guns. Maybe they were being fired by young men who were excited to have an AK-47; perhaps they were doing training drills or hunting deer in the fields outside the villages. All I knew for certain was that I had to have one.

For a young boy, I was filled with a lot of rage. I had started plotting how I would get my own back for the death of Aleer. His murder had been dealt with by way of tribal justice – the killer had been ordered to give my family some cows as compensation – but to me nothing short of the biblical eye for an eye would suffice as a just settlement of affairs. I stewed on it for years, right throughout my childhood, and I knew exactly what I was going to say to the man who stole Aleer from me before I blew his brains out: 'You killed my brother and he didn't do anything to you. He was trying to help you and you murdered him like a coward. You shot him in the back of the head. Well I am his younger brother and I have a message for you: he is waiting for you and I'm sending you there to him now.'

Boom!

I eventually left Africa without ever finding him but I kept marinating in hatred and fantasising of vengeance. Even after I was given a new life in Australia I believed that one day I would return to Sudan to carry out the sentence. Much to my dismay, I was told years later that my brother's killer didn't survive the war. The story we heard was that he died of thirst and, although I'd wanted him to have a terrible end, I was gutted by the news. I had wanted mine to be the last face he ever saw and the last voice he ever heard.

Eventually I would get to confront another nemesis from the war – a cousin of Aleer's killer, no less – and have another opportunity to vent my fury. First, though, I would have to go through several circles of hell.

3

EXODUS

Like Aleer, my big sister Aguil was educated, worldly, wise and brave. She was also politically active in the Sudanese People's Liberation Movement (SPLM) and she knew it was just a matter of time before Arab forces arrived and our village became a battlefield. By 1986, great rivers of civilians poured out of towns and villages across southern Sudan and headed to the relative safety of refugee camps in Ethiopia in the east. Aguil told Mum and our grandma to gather the entire family together and join the refugee caravans but the proud Dinka women refused to leave their lifelong home. Eventually Mum agreed that Aguil could take me with her to Ethiopia but she insisted on staying put with the rest of her children. That day I ceased to be a Dinka cattleman with dreams about great herds, lots of wives and heroic songs to sing. Instead, I became a mere droplet in a sea of refugees.

With practically no education, I could barely conceive of the world beyond our village. As Aguil and I set off in the footsteps of Aleer, all I knew was that Ethiopia was supposed to be a safe place and the people who lived there hated Arabs, too. With no shoes and just a few tattered clothes to cover us we joined the bedraggled columns of humanity trudging east out of Twic. There were hundreds of us – maybe even thousands – mostly travelling by foot. Old men and women walked alongside younger adults, kids like me and new mothers carrying hungry, crying babies. I didn't know what to make of it all, only that I was away from Mum.

The refugees were accompanied by a slow-moving convoy of military trucks heavily loaded with SPLA troops, weapons and some rations of maize, corn and water to help sustain us along the way. We were told it would be safer to travel at night, not only to avoid the sapping heat of the sun but because we had to traverse lands belonging to hostile tribes.

During the day the refugees would spread out to rest in puddles of shade beneath sparse stands of trees before setting out on the next leg of the journey late in the afternoon or at sunset. I felt reassured by the armed SPLA soldiers. They were serious-looking men who didn't seem to mess around. I looked up to them but I soon found out I wasn't the only person who secretly wished he could have one of their guns.

In a small village, just before we left Twic, a soldier was caught stealing an AK-47. Maybe he had intentions of selling it later but it didn't matter. As soon as he was found out, a senior officer in the convoy ordered his execution. A firing squad of four or five guys was assembled and on the count of three they opened fire in front of the local villagers. As the angry percussion of bullets split the air I watched the poor man drop down onto his knees and crumple to the ground, torn like a piece of meat. As horrific as it was, the episode taught me a valuable lesson which I took with me to Ethiopia: 'Never sell anything that belongs to our rebels.'

Sometimes, if the terrain and the condition of the road would allow, the trucks were loaded with some of the more frail and elderly refugees and driven up to twenty kilometres ahead. Once the human cargo was dropped at a safe location the trucks would double back and collect more of the sick and the weak, then repeat the process like a desperate game of war-zone leapfrog. Tragically, some people simply could not keep up and they fell way behind the convoy, most likely becoming prey for hyenas.

Now and then the soldiers would stop the trucks alongside the remains of animals that had been eaten by predators. If the scene of a kill was relatively fresh, they'd plunder the carcass for any remaining meat to supplement the meagre supply of grain that was keeping us all alive.

The further east we travelled, the more the landscape changed; the lush grasslands that are fed by the White Nile gave way to hotter, drier ground and scrubbier bush that was more punishing to negotiate. After a few days trudging in the harsher terrain I recycled any water I was given by drinking my own urine. Many people did.

One morning, some refugees came across what appeared to be a large piece of animal flesh on the roadside. Whatever fur and skin that had been attached to it had been scraped off leaving just meat and bone. Although they couldn't readily identify what kind of animal it had come from, the refugees judged it fresh enough to safely eat so it was cooked on an open fire. After the meat had been shared among the refugees, we pressed on.

A little further along the road, however, they came across some more random chunks of what looked like the same meat, only these were partially enclosed in black skin. Then they found part of a human hand. Then a human head. I had never been more thankful to miss out on food than I was on that day.

About a week later I was hanging off the back of one of the trucks as it lurched in the ruts of a badly potholed road when we came upon five or six giraffes grazing by the roadside. Startled by the sound of motors, the herd urgently swung their elegant necks around and took off at speed. As the gangly creatures galloped towards the safety of thicker bush, the air erupted with the staccato clatter of several AK-47s. I watched intently to see if one of the majestic animals would stagger and crash to the earth but amazingly they all seemed to get away unscathed.

The soldiers, however, knew better than to just shrug their shoulders at a lost opportunity and keep driving. They stopped the engines, watched and waited. Sure enough, within twenty minutes or so, many vultures began drawing circles in the sky about one kilometre from our position before spiralling downwards out of sight behind the treeline.

'Yeah. We got one,' a soldier said, smiling widely.

The driver took a bearing off the plunging birds and set a course through the bush. By the time we arrived, the vultures had already pecked the slain giraffe's eyeballs out of its skull and started making inroads on other soft parts of the creature's enormous fallen frame, which was pockmarked with crimson bullet holes.

When I was a younger boy in the village, Mum's twin brother Manyok had managed to kill a giraffe all by himself. Afterwards he explained the finer points of bringing down such lanky game. You can't just throw any old spear at its body and hope for the best; it needs to be a heavy spear made out of heavy wood and with a large, weighty spearhead attached. Instead of throwing it horizontally at the sides of the animal, you have to launch your spear high and vertical so the spear comes down hard into the giraffe's back. That day, Manyok only took a little meat from the giraffe; the main prize was the tail – a highly valued item Dinka people use as a necklace. Manyok sold the tail to another tribe for a great many goats. I thought of him as I watched the soldiers butcher the dead giraffe and I wondered how far the meat would go among thousands of starving refugees. Not that far, it turned out.

After what seemed like endless weeks, the caravan came to the fringe of an expanse of desert. I had never seen a landscape like it and I was stunned to learn such places existed. If there were no trees or grasses – only fine dirt – then what was the point of it? What was out there for us?

'Ethiopia,' Aguil assured me.

There was no road in the desert; we had to make our own, following in the tracks left by herds of animals. The rutted earth made walking even harder and ensured a juddering ride for anyone in the army trucks. Over the next week or so the caravan lost more sick and weak refugees on the shifting, blistering hot surface of the desert. Once again I resorted to drinking my own piss to ensure I didn't take my own place in the giant sandy graveyard.

Finally the terrain began to change and with it the weather. The desert yielded to grassland and in the distance to the east we could make out a jagged dark shape on the horizon. A day or so later we could clearly see it was a mountain range covered in deep shades of green. Ethiopia.

It grew cooler and wet, with downpours of rain that caused the trucks to slip and slide and become stuck in muddy ruts. As we climbed into the foothills near Sudan's border with Ethiopia, the vegetation grew thicker, more lush, and it teemed with wildlife unfamiliar to me: all types of monkeys and baboons and what seemed like a million noisy, brightly coloured birds. Although Ethiopia would provide us sanctuary from human predators we faced some of the same old dangers we had in Sudan, namely hyenas plus some new threats in the forms of leopards, lions and wild elephants. At the border, we crossed a river teeming with Nile crocodiles.

One threat I had always feared as a Dinka boy had

strangely disappeared during the long march out of Sudan. Along the way, many more South Sudanese blacks had joined the caravan from many different tribal areas, including my traditional foes, the Murle and the Nuer. Now that we were on the run from the common Arab threat we were no longer mortal enemies – we were fellow South Sudanese. More than that, we were fellow human beings united by the primal urge to survive.

Ethiopia's Dimma Refugee Camp was only opened by the United Nations High Commissioner for Refugees (UNHCR) in January 1986 and by the time we arrived later that year it was already home to thousands of South Sudanese seeking shelter from the war. Just a day or two's walk from the border with Sudan, Dimma wasn't much more than a sprawling village of tents and grass huts filled with scared and hungry people.

As soon as we arrived, we had to register with the UNHCR – friendly but insistent people who wanted to record our names, the villages we came from and our dates of birth. The first two questions were easy to answer but I had no idea what year I was born, let alone what day of which month. I wasn't alone. Back then, Nilotic tribal life didn't revolve around clocks and calendars, anniversaries or strict schedules. Mothers didn't note the date their children were born so there was no such thing as 'birthday' in the Dinka culture. You were simply born, you grew up, you got older and then you died.

At Dimma, though, the United Nations ran things with all the nitty-gritty fuss typical of Western culture.

They wanted a birthdate and if I couldn't supply one then they would give me one! I was assessed by a UN official who determined I was about nine years old. By this guesstimate I was born some time in 1977 but to allow for a bit of wiggle room he very kindly supplied me with the birthdate of 1 January 1977. Not only did I get to ring in each New Year hence with a bogus refugee camp birthday, I got to do it with thousands of other South Sudanese who'd been given a 1 January birthdate, too. Generally speaking, the only Dinka with real birthdays are the ones who were born in refugee camps. Western efficiency at its best! The truth is, my age is anyone's guess. I could have been born in 1976 or anytime in the 1970s. But all that really mattered as far as I could see was that I *had* been born . . . and I was still alive.

After we'd been processed we were shown the Dinka area of the camp where Aguil went about connecting with other clan members. There were some familiar faces, including a lot of women and young girls who huddled inside tents and huts, sometimes eight at a time. Although we were safer than we would have been had we stayed in Sudan, the conditions were quite poor. Just because the UN was there didn't mean people were getting enough to eat. Rations were tight and there was corruption, too. Senior people in the SPLA would often steal aid that was meant for the refugees and sell it in other parts of Ethiopia. Finding food was always a struggle, especially given that the Ethiopian famine had ended only a year earlier. No one at Dimma ever laboured to finish a meal then said, 'That's it. I've had enough.'

Apart from the early questioning about our ages, in the camp we were left to our own devices. We constructed huts out of sticks and grass and slept on the ground or in makeshift bunks made out of tree branches and bunches of grass. Some aspects of tribal life continued; clans would hold ceremonial dances and conduct tribal rituals and customs. During the day we could roam beyond the boundary but that came with risks.

The Dimma camp had been established in the heart of territory belonging to an Ethiopian tribe known for cutting the lips of girls before they got married to insert plates inside. They were also known to be angry that the UN had brought thousands of South Sudanese to live on their land.

One day I was at a small bazaar near the refugee camp when gunfire suddenly erupted around me. People started running everywhere as several men were shot dead and thudded to the ground right next to where I was standing. I took one look around at what was happening and went down as if I'd been shot, too. I lay still until the tribesmen ran back into the bush and I could hear the Ethiopians shouting that it was OK and the threat had passed. I raised myself from the dead and sped as fast as I could back to the refugee camp.

The SPLA had a presence at Dimma, too. They had training bases located nearby – another reason a lot of our food aid went missing. They also kept a prisoner at Dimma, an old Arab guy with light skin and a pure white beard. The SPLA had allowed him to set up a little shop at the camp where he sold salt, oil, clothes and various bits and pieces. In the same way I had hung around the soldiers who came to my village in Sudan, I started shadowing the old man and helping out around the shop.

I would go there every morning and find him as always, leaning on his stick. Being an Arab and a Muslim he was supposed to be my worst enemy, but I couldn't bring myself to hate him. He was harmless and he wasn't going anywhere so I would sit and listen to the stories he told in Arabic. He was a veteran of the First Sudanese Civil War and fought against the mighty Anyanya, but long before that he had owned a shop in the north.

He was a nice old guy and I liked him a lot. I would busy myself around the shop, carry things for him, run errands and do little jobs. Now and then he would give me clothes to wear. I learned a lot just by spending time with him, most importantly that you must always respect the elderly.

After more than a year in Dimma I was sent to a place called Koi River, roughly several hours' walk away, to live with my mother's younger sister, Aunty Dew. She was married to an SPLA captain named Mabior Kuir Maketh – a respected officer who was in command of a secret SPLA arms base that had recently been built. The Koi River camp was a way station and storage facility for the basic tools of warfare – machine guns, pistols, rockets, grenades, bullets, bombs and uniforms – all sourced from our allies and destined for our troops fighting in Sudan.

At that time the Ethiopian government of Mengistu Haile Mariam – a bitter enemy of the Arab government in Khartoum – supported supply bases like Koi River and other SPLA facilities set up inside their border. Along with countries such as Eritrea and Uganda, Ethiopia also helped arm the SPLA with weapons and money.

Aguil felt I would be safer at Koi River where Aunty Dew could keep an eye on me. If the aim was to shelter me from chaos and conflict, though, it didn't work. Relocating me to Koi River only fired my desire to get involved in the war. I still grieved for my slain brother and, like a lot of young tribal boys, I was filled with rage about the Arabs' destruction of my former life. I hated the fact I had been forced to run from my home and leave my mum. I didn't know if the rest of my family were even safe. Living in an army weapons base brimming with guns, my mind whirled with dreams of revenge.

There was a major SPLA training base in the region and I'd also heard about another camp where boys were being groomed into soldiers. They called it the Red Army and apparently it was just a few kilometres down the road from the Dimma Refugee Camp. I begged Aunty Dew to let me join but she flatly refused. To make matters worse, boys who were younger than me would often pass through Koi River carrying guns.

'I need to have a gun, too, Aunty Dew!' I'd whine.

'No you don't!' she'd snap.

'Those other kids have got them so they obviously need them,' I'd point out. 'That means I need one!'

'No,' she'd say. 'Forget it.'

'But I'm older than them and stronger than them!'

'I don't care.'

'Then let me join the Red Army. Everybody else is getting ready to fight and I want to fight, too.'

'No.'

'*Please!*'

'NO!'

Aunty Dew's husband Mabior was protected by a team of bodyguards, members of the SPLA's elite commandos. The same guys were also called on to serve as security whenever our leader Dr John Garang and other senior SPLA/M officials visited the base, and they were responsible for the huge cache of weapons at Koi River, too.

I shared a room with four of them, including an older soldier we called John Lokoro. The commandos took me under their wing and showed me how to clean and handle guns properly. One day I nagged John and another bodyguard named Arop Deng to let me pull the trigger of an AK-47 until they relented and took me to a makeshift firing range. Arop marked the trunk of a nearby tree with a handful of mud and showed me how to hold the rifle.

'Do it like this and point it at that tree,' he said.

The gun seemed to get heavier as I raised it to my shoulder but I also felt empowered by its shape and the feel of the steel in my hands; I felt like I was taller. I squeezed the trigger, not realising the weapon had been set to fire fully automatically. I was thrown backwards as the gun kicked and a magazine full of bullets sprayed in an arc from the tree I'd been aiming at vertically into the air. John Lokoro and the others laughed. It was a shaky start but I knew I'd be able to master it when I was given the chance.

After a year or so of hanging around at Koi River and harassing Aunty Dew she finally caved in and said I could join the Red Army. I don't know the reason for the change of heart but perhaps, since I was around twelve, I was at the age the SPLA had by then deemed acceptable for boys to be trained. Maybe I was just getting to that age when she knew she couldn't keep telling me no. In any case, I was told to go and get ready.

Aunty Dew packed some food for me – a container with a bit of peanut butter, some oil and some sugar – and I was loaded into a utility with her husband Mabior and some of his bodyguards. On the way to the Red Army base we dropped Mabior off at Dimma Refugee Camp where he was due for a meeting and the commandos continued on with me for another kilometre or so until we reached the boy soldier encampment.

Instead of being placed in a battalion to start basic training, I was taken to the camp headquarters and handed over to the leadership, clearly at Aunty Dew's request. All the senior soldiers were in their twenties and the officer in charge – a man named Chol Alue – was well aware I was related to Mabior Maketh's wife. It turned out my enrolment was conditional.

'You'll train with everybody else but you'll stay in the headquarters with us at night,' Chol told me flatly.

My first month as a boy soldier was spent sleeping in the Red Army headquarters and cooking for the trainers. I spent endless hours grinding up maize and corn, boiling water in pots and making stews. Rations were tight in the camp and even though I had access to a bit more food than the boy soldiers, who were camped in tents nearby, I was still extremely skinny and underdone. But at last I felt I was making a contribution to the war effort.

Eventually the day came when Chol was deployed with the unit of boys who were under his command. They were sent back across the border into Sudan to fight the Arabs and I was sent into the main ranks of the Red Army to continue learning how to kill.

4

LITTLE SOLDIERS

Training in how to take a person's life is as much about brainwashing as it is anything else. There's no point instructing army recruits in bush survival, combat and military strategy if you haven't taught them to robotically follow orders as well. If a person is ordered to run straight into a raging river or through a wall of fire and he simply says 'No', then what is the point of him being a soldier? Rules and orders are everything in the military – especially in an army full of frightened, flighty little boys.

I was assigned to a task force of more than one thousand child soldiers that had been given the ambitious name of Zalzal (Earthquake) Battalion 2. We were awoken at 4 am each day and put through a series of drills that wore on mercilessly until midday – with no breakfast. In the afternoon we sat through long hours of 'school' under some trees where trainers tried to teach us English. We learned the letters of the alphabet and basic words like 'hello', 'boy', 'man', 'woman', 'you', 'me'. My comprehension during these lessons was practically zero, thanks to the gruelling hours of hard physical training that preceded them.

Every day we assembled into units and marched into the surrounding hills to be drilled on how to form attacking positions, how to stand up, how to stay low, how to run, how to move in long grass, how to swim with one arm and hold our weapons high and dry in the other. We learned how to run in a zig-zag while under fire, how to dig foxholes and how to set ambushes for enemy soldiers.

Only our instructors had AK-47s so we mostly trained with sticks as stand-ins for guns. We even made stand-in noises with our mouths to indicate when we were firing our make-believe rifles and hurling pretend hand grenades as we crawled along on our bellies: 'Pa-pa-pa-pa! Coh-coh-coh-coh-coh! Zzzzzz. Bang!'

It was drummed into us that, above all else, we always had to do whatever we were told. Without question and without fail. Punishment for not complying was severe. But then, everything about the Red Army was severe. We didn't have water bottles or proper uniforms – just raggedy shorts and maybe a torn T-shirt supplied by the UN. There were no rest breaks or toilet breaks. Nor was there any leisure time and definitely no thinking for ourselves. If I was thirsty, I stayed thirsty until I nearly choked on my dry throat or until our trainers said we could all go to the river to drink together. Most of us drank our piss whenever we could.

There were no bottles of water in our tents, either. We had no mattresses or pillows – just one blanket to each boy and we slept on the ground in the filthy, ripped clothes we'd worn during the day. We couldn't spread out and we'd been told to sleep with our feet pointed at the door of the tent so if hyenas came for us in the night they'd only maul our feet, not our heads and necks, which happened to one poor boy I knew.

To answer the call of nature after dark was to take your life in your hands. The odds of getting attacked by hyenas in the bush were high enough to fire the adrenal gland. Several boys had been savaged while walking just thirty metres away to the bush for a night-time shit and were only saved by their own screams and the proximity of guards with loaded AK-47s. If ever I desperately needed to relieve myself at night I'd gather a few other boys to go with me.

'Psst. I need to take a shit,' I'd announce in the darkness. 'You can have my back and next time I'll do it for you.'

We'd arm ourselves with metal plates and rocks, not to whack hyenas or leopards with but to clang together to keep the vicious scavengers at bay long enough for us to do the deed. To endure the physical punishment of training during the day only to be confronted with an uncomfortable dirt bed and moments of sheer terror at night left me mentally exhausted. I longed for my Aunty Dew's place at Koi River and I realised I had made a terrible mistake joining the rebels.

The food was the usual bare essentials of survival: ground sorghum, maize and maybe a bit of corn.

Sometimes boys would go out and hunt so now and then there was something extra for the pot. One day I was walking down to the river to wash myself when some boys gestured to me to join them around a cooking fire. 'Ayik. Ayik, come and have some.'

I was invited to help myself to a piece of tasty meat from a steel container. Before I could have another mouthful, however, one of the boys lifted the lid off the cooking pot to reveal the head of a monkey afloat in the bubbling broth.

'What?!' I said, flustered.

'It's monkey!' the boy replied.

To me that was taboo: you might as well eat human flesh. Monkeys may be smaller but I figure we are from the same type and eating them is an abomination. I thought back to those poor people who had accidentally eaten barbecued human by the roadside on the arduous journey from Sudan.

The boys in my unit came from many different ethnic tribal groups throughout Sudan. There were Toposa and some Murle, there were boys who were Didinga, Lotuko and Nuer. Although no tensions simmered between us, there was definitely a cultural divide that took time to overcome. I did, however, have a Dinka friend – my best friend, in fact. His name was Daniel Deng Manyok.

Daniel took on his Christian name when he was baptised in a church. Just like my mum, Daniel's mother had been baptised and, as the saying goes, the blood of Christ had washed through to the rest of her family.

I felt the same way about religion as Daniel did. Although I had been born a Muslim and even had a Muslim name,

46

Abul Qasim, due to my dad's conversion, I considered it just a technical glitch – more of a paternal quirk than anything real. It never occurred to me to worship an eagle, a snake or a deer either, but when Mum explained the Christian message to me back in the village it made perfect sense. From that point I loved the God of the Bible and his son Jesus Christ, even more since the Arabs invaded and were trying to force Islam on all Sudanese.

I loved Daniel, too. He was one of those people who was just within himself. He was level-headed and always willing to help me and listen to me. Something else we shared was despair at the predicament we'd found our-selves in. After just two months of training I was over being a boy soldier and so was Daniel. I was tired of running, tired of zig-zagging, tired of being thirsty and hungry, tired of being whipped by trainers to go harder, tired of the heat, the hyenas, the shouted orders and the shit food.

With all the wisdom a thirteen-year-old boy could rely on, I decided that two months' training was quite enough preparation to go to war if it came to it. I could still carry a weapon and join the fight, just not as a member of the Red Army. I told Daniel I was planning to escape and he couldn't have been happier.

'I'm coming with you!' he declared.

Running away wasn't a novel idea. Sometimes a group of boys would slip away at night and the guards wouldn't notice until a headcount in the morning. Search parties would be dispatched but many boys fled and never returned. I didn't necessarily take that as a sign of success. If their objective was to return to their villages in Sudan then the odds were definitely against them. For starters, they would have to travel through hostile tribal lands where they would most likely be murdered. Even if they managed to tiptoe through those areas they'd have to contend with lions, leopards and hyenas.

Sometimes trainers' guns and ammunition would go missing along with some boys and I would think to myself, 'Yeah, those guys might have a chance. They might make it back to their villages.' As for the ones who left unarmed? I think a lot of those little boys, who were in need of a good feed themselves, probably ended up as meals for wild animals.

Whenever escapees were caught they'd be brought back to the camp, where they were beaten and thrown into a large, roofless makeshift prison with walls constructed from thorny tree branches – punishment for breaking the army's golden rule: 'Do as you are told.'

Daniel and I weren't too concerned about being murdered, eaten alive or captured because we weren't planning on making a long-distance run back to Sudan. Our cunning plan was to head to the Dimma Refugee Camp instead and simply melt into the crowd. Daniel's mum lived at Dimma with his four sisters and younger brother so we figured that's where we'd go.

The escape itself was easy. We waited until the blanket of night had fallen and, clutching metal plates and rocks, we walked out of the camp and along the dirt road towards Dimma, about a kilometre away. We weren't dressed in uniforms, just rags, so there was nothing to suggest we were AWOL child soldiers. To the average person we were just skinny refugee boys adrift in the African night and far from home.

We felt safe in Daniel's mum's hut and stayed there for the night. The next day I was shocked to see how big Dimma had grown since I'd left, and still people continued to pour in. Noisy trucks rattled into the camp continually, even at night, and they trailed long ribbons of exhausted, emaciated refugees. When I looked into their haunted faces I recognised all the emotions I felt after I'd staggered some three hundred kilometres across Sudan.

Although Daniel and I were cautious and on edge at first, our plan of disappearing into the crowds at Dimma seemed to have worked. No one appeared to be looking for us so I spent time with Daniel and his family, and explored the camp looking for extra sources of food. Aguil had long since left Dimma and – as with the rest of my direct family – I had no idea where she was. The way I figured it, if I was still alive then there was a good chance they were still alive, too.

After a few days I started to think I'd never have to worry about the Red Army again and ceased looking over my shoulder. Then one morning, at about 4 am, I heard voices whispering in Arabic outside Daniel's family hut.

'You go that way and I'll wait here, OK?' a man said. 'But do it quietly.'

I didn't pay any attention and rolled over to go back to sleep but moments later, a group of soldiers stormed into the hut clutching clumps of burning grass to light their way. Daniel and I were dragged outside and, after our hands were tied, we were pushed to the ground and whipped with a cane.

The Red Army guards had seen it all before. They knew to leave it a few days before launching a search party; by then, runaway boys like us would have let their defences down and become easy pickings. We were marched back to the camp where we would soon learn the consequences of breaking the army's golden rule.

—

Anyang was a Dinka boy. At sixteen, he was considered a relatively senior recruit in the Red Army and had been promoted to the position of the camp's prison warden. He was solid and tall, with a face that seemed permanently twisted into a scowl. Unlike the newer boys, Anyang wore camouflage army fatigues and usually had an AK-47 slung over his shoulder on a strap. He was clothed in so much power that part of me fleetingly wished I could become like him when I finished my training. It was a short-lived ambition.

Anyang ordered some of the teenage guards under his command to throw Daniel and me into the bush prison, along with some other boys who'd been rounded up too. It was a haphazard-looking structure that resembled a giant, spiky birdcage. Since it had no roof there was nowhere to take shelter from the sun during the day or when cold rain fell in the night. Our cries for water were ignored and after several hours I started to panic, scared I might literally die of thirst. Only when the sun was at its highest and hottest did Anyang decide it was time to get down to business.

We were marched down to the river that flowed past the camp, dunked into the water and ordered back up the bank. There we were told to roll across the burning hot sand with our hands clamped between our legs – thirty metres one way then thirty metres back, over and over again. When our clothes were finally bone dry we were hogtied so the real punishment could begin. Anyang made sure we were bound so tightly – at our wrists, ankles and our elbows – that being tied up was agonising punishment in itself. When I moved even one centimetre the rope cut like a knife into my skin.

I heard the whip a millisecond before it ripped into my flesh. When Anyang raised his arm and brought the first blow down onto my back, his cane made a sharp humming noise as it cut through the hot, tropical air. *Whoop!* And then *CRACK!* From that moment the only sound I heard for the next hour was screaming: my screams, other boys' screams and Anyang screaming at us.

The pain was excruciating, so far beyond anything I had ever felt that I could hardly process it. I guess that's what torture is: pain on top of unbearable pain. When it was finally over we were dragged away and thrown into the jail of thorns like we were shit.

I was imprisoned for the next two weeks and made to pound grain, fetch firewood and cook for the prison guards. A few weeks after I was released to resume training, however, I was ready to run away again. Each time I ran, usually to Dimma, I vowed to be more careful and strategic. Sometimes I would be gone for a few days and other times for a week or more – but I was always caught.

After a while I realised the search parties never looked in tents where women and girls were sleeping so I began sleeping in tents between girls I knew from my clan until the guards twigged to the subterfuge.

Each time the torture seemed worse than the last, maybe because I knew what to expect and the fear and dread put my pain receptors on high alert. Or maybe it really *did* get worse as my nonstop disobedience stoked my superiors into a greater rage. Sometimes Anyang ordered the punishment to begin at 4 am. I'd be made to stand on one leg for what seemed like hours and I was whipped if the other foot touched the ground. I'd be tied up again and flogged until I passed out. Forty lashes. Fifty lashes! Then I was forced to roll in the dirt like an animal.

I hated Anyang and the Red Army so much that as soon as I had recovered I would run away again. I even managed to escape from the prison. In the dead of night the prison guards would be asleep so I would quietly dig underneath the branches that formed the walls. I wasn't much more than skin and bones so I didn't need much space to wriggle through and head for Dimma again, bleeding from where the thorns had torn my flesh open.

I sometimes considered running all the way back to Koi River and Aunty Dew but that journey would take far longer and I feared being eaten by hyenas or leopards, or shot by the local tribesmen along the way. Instead of hiding in tents with friends or family at Dimma, I took to sleeping among the branches at the tops of trees. Eventually, though, I would grow complacent and soon be back on terra firma sleeping between some female cousins. 'They're not looking for me anymore,' I would tell myself. But they always were.

I would sometimes abscond with Daniel, sometimes on my own and sometimes I would make a run for it with another kid from the Red Army camp. There was always someone as desperate as I was to escape. By the time Anyang started rubbing chilli powder into our wounds I was ready to murder him. I used to daydream about it. First I would torture him for a day or so with sticks and fire and then I would kill him. He had never made any attempts to treat my injuries; instead he made a full and focused effort to ensure the pain and suffering was as bad as it could be. In my eyes he was evil and the world would be a better place without him.

I still grieve for one poor child who was tied up tight at his elbows for several days. By the time anyone realised his arms were literally dying on his body it was too late. When he was finally sent to the camp hospital the only option was to amputate both his arms.

I thought Anyang was as cunning as he was brutal. Sometimes when he was making us run or stand on one leg he would take the AK-47 off his shoulder and lean it against a tree. When I knew he wasn't looking at me, my eyes would be drawn hungrily to the weapon.

What if I ran over, picked it up and shot him dead right now? I'd think. I would get a bad punishment for sure but I don't care. He deserves to die. But what if it's a trick? What if he put the gun down as a test to see if I would try to pick it up? And what if I did and when I pulled the trigger there were no bullets in the magazine? That would just give him a reason to torture me even more. Why else would he just leave the gun there? It *has* to be a trick.

I'd look at Anyang but his dark eyes never betrayed his secrets.

—

When I wasn't on the run or being subjected to torture I actually received training in the Red Army. Despite my best efforts not to be one, over the course of eight months I slowly learned how to be a soldier. I became proficient in battlecraft and how to move and survive in combat situations. I had learned how to launch assaults and ambushes, and I had even learned how to lay the fallen to rest.

Our camp was in the heart of what was then known as the Third World; we had limited access to clean water and virtually no sanitation. Consequently, disease ran rife. Sometimes boys would die in the camp hospital and others would be found dead in tents or little huts.

A lot of boys succumbed to malaria and dysentery but some children shot themselves accidentally while learning how to clean guns, including a close friend of mine. There was no one to help us except for one nurse named

Adhardid, but we called her Mamma Ring. She lived at Dimma and periodically treated boys who had contracted disease or hurt themselves during training. Mamma Ring tended to child soldiers from other camps, too. She was like a mother to hundreds of helpless boys and she saved a lot of lives.

Some children, however, were beyond help. Like me, a lot of boys never realised how hard the training would be or how much they would miss their families and yearn for their mums and dads. Some felt it would be better just to die so they committed suicide.

If a boy in our battalion didn't wake up in the morning we figured out which tribe he was from, so later on the elders in his village could be informed. The trainers would write his name down, making sure there was a record that he had indeed lived and died in the Red Army camp. Then other boy soldiers would be ordered to bury him. We'd wrap his body in his sheet and carry him into the bush and dig his grave – maybe half a metre deep. After that, the boy basically ceased to exist.

Every night I begged God not to assign me to the ranks of dead soldier boys. I wanted to live because I wanted to kill. Another thing I had learned in the Red Army was how to hate, how to stew in rage and lust after vengeance. As my training came to an end I was primed to unleash my wrath upon the enemy – but not the one I had been taught to destroy.

All I needed was to be deployed in the same unit as Anyang. As soon as I was alone with him on the battlefield he was as good as dead. Only after I had dispatched him to the fires of hell in a hail of bullets would I be able to concentrate on fighting the war against the Arabs.

5

REBEL, REBEL

The very moment I was handed a gun of my own I felt invincible.

The rebel leader Dr John Garang had arrived at the Red Army camp amid a phalanx of bodyguards to address our battalion. We had graduated from training with sticks and were ready to kill the Arabs with bullets. But first, we had to sit for hours in the hot sun as Dr Garang and other SPLA officials droned on and on about the fight for South Sudanese independence and the vital role we all had to play in the noble and historic struggle. For such a simple message they never seemed to run out of things to say about it. We sat there so long I pissed in my pants, confident I would be dry by the time the speeches finished.

When Dr Garang's convoy finally departed we were each given an AK-47 and a khaki-coloured camouflage uniform. Now that we were dressed the part and armed to the teeth we really *were* rebel soldiers. As my hands explored the Russian-made assault rifle I felt like I had real power for the very first time in my life.

Because my father had died when I was young, nobody paid much attention to me. Now and then I'd overhear snippets of conversation that gave me clues about my lack of status:

'Who is that boy, Ayik Chut? Who is his father?'

'He has no father. His father died.'

'Oh.'

The way I understood it, I was a bit of a nobody. In Dinka culture, to lose your father is to lose part of your place in the world; a little bit of your own dignity and respect disappears with the dead. Because I was unmoored in this way I was more of an afterthought to anyone outside of my clan. Then people like Anyang felt they could push me around with impunity. Well, now I had a gun, and no one was going to treat me like shit ever again. That night I begged God again to please, *please* deploy me alongside Anyang.

Much to my annoyance it wasn't God but Aunty Dew who intervened in my destiny. As she had done when I first entered the Red Army headquarters, she had pulled strings to make sure her big sister's little boy would be all right. While Anyang and hundreds of others, including my best friend Daniel, were sent back to Sudan to take the fight to the enemy, I grudgingly accepted my posting to the commando unit at Koi River. Instead of killing Anyang I would instead help oversee the flow of guns and munitions, and serve as a bodyguard whenever Dr Garang and other SPLA leaders were in town.

The one good thing about Koi River was it was bursting at the seams with firearms. If ever I wanted to change my gun I could walk into a giant shed packed to the rafters with AK-47s and take my pick. All I had to do was tell the manager, 'I want a new one,' and he'd take my old gun, mark it down in some paperwork and I could select a brand-new assault rifle right off the shelf. I loved the oily smell of a brand-new gun.

AK-47s weren't the only things we had in bulk storage. There were sheds full of all types of hand grenades, rocket-propelled grenades, heavy machine guns, landmines, combat boots, eight-shot automatic pistols, uniforms and crate upon crate of every kind of ammunition an army could wish for. The cache must have been worth millions of dollars.

Still, the Kalashnikov remained my favourite weapon and I particularly liked the model that featured a metal folding stock instead of the standard fixed shoulder stock. It meant I could shorten the overall length of the weapon, making it easier for a little guy like me to carry, hide and fire.

Access to guns wasn't the only benefit of being based at Koi River. Since I was a close relative of the commander's wife (who I was beginning to realise had a lot of influence), John Lokoro and the other commandos were generally good to me. I was also allowed certain privileges, like being able to disappear for a few weeks at a time to visit my sister Aguil, who had returned to Dimma. I had other family there, too, including my beloved young cousin Ruben and his extended family.

The population at Dimma continued to balloon and it now resembled a sprawling town with dirt streets that wound through a mini-metropolis crowded with grass huts of varying sizes. It had become home to many people – home in the truest sense because they had nowhere else to go. Dimma crawled with people from every tribe and every age group, from newborns to the white-haired elderly.

With so many mouths to feed, the UN rations were augmented by people hunting and foraging for their own food. There were other SPLA soldiers and child soldiers in and around Dimma, and often they'd go into the nearby hills and mountains with their machine guns to stalk rabbits, monkeys, antelope and little African deer called dik-diks.

The Ethiopian landscape was different from my Dinka homeland. The steep shoulders of mountainsides were draped in lush shawls of jungle that were home to all manner of fruit-covered trees. Unlike people from other tribal groups, I still refused to eat monkey. Instead I made a habit of watching and learning from them, and after a while I figured whatever fruit the monkeys ate I would eat too.

One day I decided to try to trap a hyena – not that I would ever put the filthy flesh in my mouth, since they feed on long-dead animals – but more for the pure sport of it. I got my hands on a pig hoof, which I used for bait. I dug a hole in the bush just outside the Koi River base and set a snare using a flexible branch bent over to the ground until it was under high tension with a loop of wire attached to it. The idea was that when a hyena came for the pig hoof it would trigger the snare, the flexible stick would suddenly snap upright, the wire noose would pull tight around the thing's neck and in the morning there would be a dead hyena dangling in the air. It worked the very first time I tried it.

Feeling very pleased with myself, I couldn't wait to tell the other commandos, even though I knew I had committed a serious offence. My Aunty Dew's husband's name was Mabior Kuir Maketh. In his lineage, a hyena was called kuir. Within each clan, there is a lineage and they each have their own gods: snakes, eagles, bulls, birds.

'Hey, I caught a hyena last night,' I bragged to John Lokoro, 'but I don't want my aunty or her husband to know because the hyena is his god.'

'You did what?' said John, sounding alarmed.

'Yeah, yeah! I trapped a hyena, right over there,' I said pointing towards the bush.

'Oh no, no, no, no,' he groaned, shaking his head. Thankfully John never told anyone about my god-killing exploits and even helped me untangle the dead deity from the snare and drag its corpse away from the base so nobody could see what I had done.

'If you kill a hyena again,' he warned, pressing his index finger into my chest, 'you'll be in real trouble.'

One day some other child soldiers attacked a leopard and her cubs. They chased the mother away and shot the defenceless cubs, except for one, which they delivered as a gift to Dr John Garang. For the first six months of its life the cub travelled with the rebel leader on tours of bases and camps as he oversaw the war effort. However, the leopard's job as a glorious war-time mascot came to an end after it started to attack people.

John Garang's security guards had built a wooden cage for the big cat and although it was well fed, the thing was totally nuts – as any wild predator would be if it was raised in that fashion by creatures it saw as dinner. Even so, some of Dr Garang's bodyguards sometimes let it out of the cage and tried to play with it. After it mauled a couple of his most trusted guys, the leopard was reassigned to Koi River, where it became the pet of our commando unit.

Because you can't just open a tin of Whiskas and put it in front of a leopard, the two other bodyguards and I would go off and hunt monkeys to feed it. Since we didn't have an enemy to shoot at, we would blast away at Ethiopia's wildlife whenever we got the chance. With all that gunfire going on, the area around Koi River started to run empty of larger prey; the elephants, antelope, buffalo and the larger deer all ran away. But not the monkeys – they're cheeky little things and they think they're smart. If I fired at a monkey and missed, it would scurry into the trees nearby. But in much the same way that I'd get complacent after a few days in hiding from the Red Army guards, five minutes later it would be back on the same branch and picking at the same piece of fruit thinking it had shown me who was boss. Consequently, shooting monkeys in trees was like shooting fish in a barrel.

With its steady, lazy diet of monkey meat, the leopard

grew and grew. Within a year it was enormous and although it was spoiled it was just as crazy as ever. It had been attacked by hyenas when it was a cub, which only served to make it even twitchier. To prevent such a mauling happening again, we made a bed for it in a tree. We gave the leopard enough rope so it could climb into the branches at night and out of range of hyenas. That length of rope also determined the invisible circumference around the tree where you could safely walk. Everyone at Koi River knew the point at which you had to stop before you fell within the leopard's striking distance.

One afternoon I was sitting around playing a traditional card game with some other guys – a good ten metres away from the invisible circle – when we were joined by a young soldier named Bul Aguang. I'd never seen him before; he was from another base nearby but for whatever reason he just turned up that day and put his gun in a nearby hut.

We were all having a good time, excited about the game and laughing at jokes when the air was suddenly ripped open by a terrible scream. We all turned as one to see the leopard up on its hind legs and its jaw clamped around Bul Aguang's throat. Within a second or two I grabbed my gun and took aim at the thrashing tangle of cat and boy in front of me.

'Don't shoot! Don't shoot!' a voice screamed out above the chaos. 'Don't shoot! Turn the gun around!'

It was one of the older commandos. He picked up a large stick, ran towards the leopard and belted it hard. The giant cat momentarily let go of Bul Aguang, long enough for the rest of us to drag him into safe territory. The whole thing was over in about twenty seconds but the damage to Bul Aguang was severe. As he lay in the dirt, his eyes wide with terror, large bubbles of blood inflated and fell every time he drew a sharp, gargling breath. On top of the heavy blood loss from the hole in his throat, Bul Aguang didn't seem to be getting enough air.

There was only one nurse at Koi River. He looked at Bul Aguang and said the boy needed much more help than he could provide. Once we'd bandaged his throat as best we could we loaded him into a truck and he was driven to Dimma, where proper white people's doctors from the UN could treat him. We had no idea if he would live or die.

Despite what I had suffered in the Red Army training camp and the trauma I still felt about being separated from my mum, I managed some moments of happiness during my time at Koi River. After we fled Sudan, I figured my dreams of becoming a great Dinka singer were pretty much dead. I had no herd of cows to sing songs about so there was no point. But when I was in Dimma I met a one-legged Dinka man named Hakim who taught me to play a traditional harp-like guitar called a rababa and all of a sudden I had music back in my heart.

'If I can't be a Dinka singer I might be able to entertain people by playing this thing,' I mused as Hakim showed me how to coax melodies from the rababa's five strings. I got to be pretty good at it and was invited to join a musical group led by a soldier named Napoleon. We were sometimes called

on to entertain officials at Dimma and, although I wasn't
front and centre like Napoleon, I cherished the opportunity
to sing and play.

Whenever I performed I felt a surge of happiness.
Using a mixture of Arabic and Dinka language we sang
love songs and spirited anthems about the war and the
nobility of defending our traditional lands. I even wrote
a few songs of my own about the conflict and the great
Dr Garang. The song I liked the most, however, was sung
from the perspective of a young Arab fighter from the north:

My father told me, 'Don't become a soldier
If you join the army you will have to fight Dinka
And if you fight Dinka, ohh that isn't good for you
To fight Dinka is to throw yourself into fire.'

Our musical group wasn't the only entertainment at
Dimma. One night outside Dr John Garang's house, I saw
a television for the first time. The SPLA set the thing up in
the bush using a noisy generator for power. It was a black-
and-white set about the size of a modern microwave and
I couldn't quite work out how all those people fit inside it.

Aptly, the movie was *Commando*, starring the great
Arnold Schwarzenegger, although I didn't know it was a
'movie'. I had no concept of films or TV, Hollywood stars,
special effects, stuntmen or extras; I thought Arnold was a
real commando who was capable of super-human feats of
strength. And he was so tough! Whenever he was injured he
never so much as winced with pain let alone screamed his
lungs out like Bul Aguang had done.

Dozens of soldiers crowded around as Arnold's heroics

flickered out of the strange box. Being a little kid I wasn't tall enough to get a decent view. Not willing to miss a moment of it, I climbed onto the lower branches of a nearby tree with some other boys, where we sat spellbound for the next hour and a half. That must all be happening now in that different world Mum told me about, I thought as white people fired guns at each other from speeding cars inside the TV.

The film hadn't been overdubbed from English so hardly any of the younger soldiers had a clue what Arnold was saying, but in testament to the storytelling power of Tinseltown I actually had a pretty good handle on what was going on: basically, Arnold was trying to save his little girl from a bunch of bad guys who'd stolen her away from him. It was hard to believe such an enormous man even existed. Arnold's muscles were twice as big as any I'd seen on men in Africa. I couldn't imagine what he must eat every day. And he was brave, too. Arnold risked his life in the most amazing acts of daring, and each new move drew gasps and great cheers of approval from the tired, skinny commandos hunkered there in the wilds of Ethiopia.

At one point Arnold jumped from the landing gear of a passenger jet that had just taken off. 'AAARRGGHH!' we cried and held our breath as he fell towards certain death. Miraculously, though, Arnold landed feet-first in a swamp with a great splash only to stand straight back up and get after the bad guys again. More wild cheering drifted across the African night.

At the end of the film, when Arnold saved his little girl by obliterating all the bad guys in a hail of bullets and impaling the arch-villain on a steam pipe, some of the soldiers leaped to their feet and shot their guns approvingly up at the stars. It had been a night to remember.

We didn't know it then but soon the only bullets to be fired in Dimma would be incoming.

—

The government of Mengistu Haile Mariam had started to crumble. He'd taken control of Ethiopia as the head of a military junta in 1977 but democratic rebels had waged an insurgency for years in an attempt to overthrow him. In 1991 a coalition called the Ethiopian People's Revolutionary Democratic Front (EPRDF) succeeded. As Mengistu was pulled down, so was the cloak of protection he had thrown around the SPLA as we fought our own civil war across the border. Almost overnight the tables turned and all Sudanese were driven out of Ethiopia, including the refugees.

It started with rumours. I'd wake in the morning at Koi River and hear that a town a thousand kilometres away had been taken over by EPRDF forces. The next day we'd get news another village had fallen, closer to us this time. Before long, apprehension gave way to panic as the distant but unmistakable echoes of war drifted in from over the horizon. The commandos at Koi River got a certain look in their eye that said, 'They're coming.'

Aunty Dew told me to go ahead to Dimma and find Aguil and the rest of my family but by the time I got there it was too late: virtually all the refugees had already fled in the direction of Sudan. My family was nowhere to be seen. As the giant camp emptied out, the SPLA destroyed everything that remained; the huts, food stores, buildings and machinery were torched to prevent them falling into the hands of the EPRDF. As the last of us stumbled out of the burning camp we could hear rocket launchers being fired back at Koi River and I knew my team wouldn't last long there before the Ethiopians arrived.

The commandos at Koi River set fire to everything they were unable to take with them, too: the enormous cache of weapons and munitions, cars that weren't going to make it through the terrain, food supplies, machinery, huts and buildings. All of it went up in towering, twisting columns of black smoke.

We also had to leave some people behind; the elderly, frail and sick who couldn't make a run for it were forced to remain and throw themselves onto the mercy of the Ethiopians. Among them was Hakim, the one-legged man who'd taught me to play the rababa. God knows what happened to him.

Amid the thud of nearby bombs and the scream of approaching rockets, it was clear the Ethiopians didn't just want us to leave the camps – they wanted us out of their country altogether. They chased us, firing, all the way to the fast-moving river that snakes along that part of Ethiopia's border with Sudan.

The EPRDF was a well-equipped conquering army, whereas we only had the guns and ammunition we could carry. As their RPGs and tracer rounds tore through the air just above our heads we prepared to take to the water and swim for the safety of the Sudanese town of Raad on the opposite bank.

Many boy soldiers had come from the ethnic Nuba tribes who made their homes in the mountains of central Sudan. Because they were highland people they hadn't grown up surrounded by creeks and rivers and consequently they never learned to swim. That day I saw a lot of them drown.

I jumped in and swam back to Sudan with one arm while holding my weapon out of the water with the other. With every stroke I expected powerful reptilian jaws to crush my legs and pull me under in a death roll. Somehow I made it across alive.

As I stood sodden on the bank I locked eyes with a boy who was flailing about fifteen metres from shore. I wanted to jump back in and help him, but we were still under fire from the EPRDF. I turned my back on him for a moment to dodge another bullet but when I turned again he was gone. I didn't know if he'd been dragged down by the swirling currents or a crocodile – I just knew mine was the last face he ever saw.

That moment would press down hard on me for years to come; I felt like a weight that would never be lifted had been placed on my back. That boy's loved ones would probably never know what happened to him, whereas I would never forget.

Some other boys who couldn't swim made the crossing on a bulldozer they'd found on the Ethiopian side of the river. When an SPLA soldier started the engine, he had to raise the bulldozer blade off the ground in order to get the lumbering machine moving. As hydraulics shifted the big steel arms that held the blade, one of the boys became trapped across his upper thigh. Hideously compressed in the steel pincer, he screamed all the way as the dozer carried the frightened boys across the river to relative safety.

When they reached land the blade was lowered and the wounded boy flopped to the ground in front of me with his right leg dangling by a thread of skin. His scrotum had been torn open and his testicles were hanging out. I didn't see him take his last breath but my guess is he bled to death a short time later.

It was late afternoon by the time we started to regroup in Raad. A few bright red tracer rounds intermittently fizzed overhead in the gloaming but most of the Ethiopians' heavy shelling had stopped. They had accomplished what they'd come to do and as the last guns fell silent we took stock of the changes in our fortunes. We may have been back home, but our country was awash with blood.

6

KAPOETA

I had only been back in Sudan for a few hours before I was invited to commit mass murder.

Shaken and exhausted after the terrifying escape from Ethiopia, thousands of refugees and more than one thousand SPLA rebels did their best to reconnect and reorganise at a makeshift camp that had quickly sprung up on the outskirts of Raad. The SPLA controlled the town of Raad and they even had a group of North-Sudanese Arab prisoners of war locked up in the town's jail – a real prison with walls and bars. Later that night, a rebel soldier I knew named Dhieu Abuk asked me if I wanted to go for a drive along the river.

'What do you mean "go for a drive to the river?"' I asked, confused, considering what we'd just been through there.

'We have a truck full of prisoners of war and we're driving them somewhere,' Dhieu replied evasively.

'Where are you driving them?' I pressed.

'About an hour that way along the river,' he said, vaguely waving a skinny arm towards the south.

'Why?' I asked.

'We're going to kill them all, Ayik,' Dhieu finally said in a conspiratorial voice. 'It's thought the Ethiopians might cross the river tonight and attack, and if they do they might release the Arab prisoners, who might try to kill us too.'

War is a tangled, messy business that presents a catalogue of moral, ethical, legal, spiritual and humanitarian dilemmas almost every day. At the top of the list is the fundamental dictum of war: kill or be killed. Although Dhieu and the other SPLA executioners might have felt justified, the idea of taking the lives of unarmed people deeply disturbed me.

I was happy to fight for our independence – to kill other human beings in order to save our people and our villages from invaders who were trying to kill us. But shooting unarmed fighters who had already been caught was wrong on every level. To me it was the same as killing an elderly person, like the white-haired Arab POW I had befriended at Dimma. He wasn't a threat to anyone, so the way I saw it, he was no different to the Muslim men cowering in the back of Dhieu's truck with their wrists bound.

'We're going to line them up on the riverbank, shoot them all and throw the bodies in for the crocodiles to eat,' Dhieu continued. 'Are you coming?'

'No, Dhieu,' I said quietly. 'I'm not.'

We remained in Raad for several weeks while an existing camp was expanded to accommodate the refugees.

The new camp had none of the medical support or food aid we'd had in Dimma. The tents had been hastily erected and the grass huts were nothing more than circular walls and roofs quickly thrown together as emergency shelters.

Now that we were back in Sudan, some of the refugees felt they were safer than they had been in Dimma. After all, they had been chased out of Ethiopia at gunpoint. Time would show it was a misplaced sense of security. Absolutely nobody was safe in Sudan. We weren't even safe from each other.

While we camped south of Raad I caught up with some Red Army soldiers I had trained with. We were all a bit older by now – fourteen, fifteen and sixteen – and the more senior guys who had trained us were fully grown men. With so many boys surging blindly through puberty and their young-adult superiors looking to bend the world to their will, the SPLA ranks were a testosterone-fuelled time bomb. Add in the fact we were perpetually fatigued, stressed, hungry and traumatised, and it's no wonder tensions sometimes reached breaking point.

One morning an argument erupted between two guys I knew pretty well – a boy soldier and one of our more senior ex-trainers. I wasn't close enough to the hut they were in to overhear what they were fighting about but it definitely escalated quickly. In the next moment a single gunshot rang out. The boy soldier had drawn his pistol and shot his superior in the head at point-blank range.

A deathly hush fell after the first shot and then *BANG!* – a second gunshot was heard. It was the sound of the boy putting the gun under his chin and committing suicide. When we rushed in to see what had happened we found him lying dead in the dirt, a lake of blood around his head and the gun dangling from his limp hand. We were surprised to hear someone moaning. When he'd shot his superior, the boy soldier obviously hadn't aimed straight enough because the poor man was still alive – gravely injured with a bullet hole in his head, but somehow still breathing. We tried to nurse him as best we could but after thirty minutes he caught up with his little executioner by dying too.

The tragedy laid bare the cold reality that in war, the gun is everything. It didn't matter whether you were a boy soldier, a tank commander, a great general or a tribesman in the bush – if one pulls his gun first and shoots the other, then that is the end of that. On this occasion the lesson was even clearer because the only thing to survive intact and functioning was the instrument of death itself. The gun was the only victor that day. It *was* everything.

The murder–suicide also raised the question of what the war was doing to children like us. Even after shooting a superior, that boy hadn't needed to put a bullet in his own head. Back in those days in the tribe you could kill someone and only pay for it by way of compensation. In the army if you killed someone like that you might only do a few years in jail.

So why did a young boy wake up one day, shoot a superior and then commit suicide? I knew the answer to the first part because I still planned to kill Anyang and the coward who had shot my brother years earlier. In an amazing coincidence I had learned they were distant relatives. But I had no intention of killing myself after dispatching them. To me then, that would have been a sign of serious mental health problems. Indeed it would be almost a full year before I contemplated my own act of murder–suicide.

—

Not long after those comrades died in a hut outside Raad I was born again. A Christian minister prayed with me beneath the boughs of a large tree in the refugee camp and dabbed my head with water. I took the Christian name Daniel – not to honour the hero of the biblical book that carries his name, but out of love for my friend Daniel Deng Manyok. On the day that I took a share in his name I prayed that God would keep him safe wherever he was. In war you need every bit of help you can get.

Many months after we were kicked out of Ethiopia we received orders to travel several hundred kilometres south to a town called Kapoeta in a region closer to Sudan's borders with Uganda and Kenya. The two-to-three-week trek from Raad to Kapoeta was like a re-run of the refugee caravan Aguil and I had joined when we fled Twic for Ethiopia five years earlier. There were a few army trucks but most of the refugees travelled on foot. The biggest difference was that this time I was one of the soldiers and I had a gun.

The journey was long, hot and exhausting, and it was fraught with the usual dangers inherent in travelling through other people's lands. In this case, the territory of the Toposa people. Although the Toposa had sometimes been inclined to back the SPLA, they supported Sudanese government troops, too. At the end of the day, the Toposa threw their support behind whichever side gave them the most food or weapons. They were not to be trusted or meddled with.

Even though I was almost always armed I still felt vulnerable, particularly when nature called – and not only because of the threat of hyenas. The danger with having a shit in Toposa country was twofold: first, you had to separate yourself from your group and second, you had to separate yourself from your weapon in order to do your business.

The safe tribal practice of going to the toilet as a group wasn't enforced in the Red Army, mostly because our superiors didn't care about us the way our families did. It was frighteningly common for Toposa to sneak up behind shitting boy soldiers and crack them hard across the back of the neck with a heavy club. The boy would fall forwards from his haunches, temporarily paralysed, his gun would quietly be taken and then he'd be finished off with repeated blows to the skull. The stealthy attacks were hard to defend against and often the victims weren't found until another member of their unit went for a number two. Sometimes soldiers just went to the toilet and were never seen again.

These ambushes, plus the return to the homelands of deserting child soldiers, allowed tribal groups throughout Sudan to arm themselves against everyone they considered an enemy. Many tribesmen had volunteered to train with the SPLA just so they could get their hands on weapons and then promptly desert. This was more common among ethnic groups who were traditional Dinka enemies. Since the rebel leader John Garang was a Dinka man they didn't necessarily trust the SPLA or see the quest for South Sudanese independence through the same lens as we Dinka did. That's not to say Dinka fighters didn't desert, too, but the loyalty we felt to Dr Garang and the sense of honour and duty among families and clans definitely made it easier to stay.

Late one afternoon, one of our vehicles broke down and I was stranded with six or seven other soldiers near a village north of Kapoeta. We decided it was best to go and talk to the local Toposa and explain why we were in their territory and smooth out any misunderstandings. That evening we met with one of young tribesman and told him we were helping the refugees, fighting against the Arab aggressors and we were not there to take advantage of the Toposa in any way. As a gesture of goodwill I gave him five or six bullets from my magazine.

We retreated to where we'd dug ourselves in outside of the village and tried to get some rest. A few hours later, just as I was drifting off to sleep, the tribesman came from the village and spoke to us in a whisper.

'You were good to give me some bullets and I am grateful,' he said. 'But I am telling you now that if you go to sleep here you will not wake up.'

Without another word he disappeared back into the darkness. Knowing our lives were at risk, we decided the best way to slip out of the area quietly and without being spotted was to leave one by one and regroup several hundred metres down the road.

Within thirty minutes we'd made good our escape and as we crept along under the stars until dawn all I could think was, What if I hadn't given that guy the bullets? It's likely we would have had our skulls crushed and been left for the vultures. It was the first time I'd ever seen bullets save lives. It was the last time, too.

—

Kapoeta was a dusty garrison town in Namorunyang State in the south-eastern corner of Sudan. The SPLA had taken it from Khartoum's army in 1988 so our unit fell in with the rebels who were already stationed there. Meanwhile, the refugees who'd come south from Raad with us joined the other displaced women, children and elderly who were camped in the dirt on another fringe of the town.

After about two weeks in Kapoeta I was relieved and overjoyed to find my sisters Aguil and Yar sheltering in the town along with my cousin Ruben and other members of my family. To everyone's relief, the UNHCR had set up operations to help look after the hordes who poured into Kapoeta day and night. While I was happy some of my loved ones were still alive I had no idea about the fate of Mum and my younger siblings. As ever, I prayed that God would look after them the way He seemed to be watching over the rest of us. I was also pleased to briefly run into

Bul Aguang, the unlucky guy I'd helped save from the jaws of our leopard.

Ever since I'd paid for my life with bullets I realised ammunition had become a valuable currency in Sudan, so when the local Toposa came to us with milk and meat to trade I was happy to quietly slip a few shiny AK-47 rounds into their hands. By doing so I was breaking the rule I had laid down for myself years earlier after watching the SPLA firing squad kill the gun thief on the trek to Ethiopia: 'Never sell anything that belongs to our rebels.' Now that I *was* a rebel I had adjusted the rule: 'Never get caught selling anything that belongs to our rebels.' Besides, I told myself, a few bullets here and there in exchange for food wouldn't hurt.

The township of Kapoeta was built on harsh, arid land. Water had to be hauled up from deep wells and trees (and thus firewood) were scarce. The township was surrounded by small, thorny bushes and in order to cook we had to roam quite far in search of dry wood. More often than not, the Toposa were out there waiting for us.

We lost many child soldiers in the simple quest to find cooking fuel, and soon we only ever went out to collect firewood in large, armed groups. But since nature called us at different times we couldn't go to the toilet as a squad, so the Toposa remained a constant threat through their favourite tactic of ambushing lone soldiers with clubs.

Our people were getting picked off in the bush every day but *still* I gave the Toposa my bullets. I never considered the prospect that those same 7.62 mm rounds would ultimately be given back to me and my comrades at deadly velocity. All I cared about was that the ammo afforded me some meat – a genuine luxury in times of war. I was so grateful to be eating something other than maize and sorghum that I didn't even question what kind of meat the Toposa were giving us. For all I knew, it was donkey or – even worse – dog, but at that stage I didn't care.

Emboldened by my small-scale black marketeering I started trading magazines full of ammo for bigger cuts of mystery meat and Toposa milk. I wasn't the only one doing it and I knew other people were committing higher crimes; some even stole guns and sold them to the Toposa before disappearing back to their own tribe or crossing into Kenya or Uganda and the safety of a refugee camp.

Sometimes I thought about deserting, too. An AK-47 was worth around twelve thousand Kenyan shillings on the black market – a hell of a lot of money. But, being a good Dinka boy, I didn't want to let down my Aunty Dew, Dr John Garang or my family – nor did I fancy being lined up in front of everyone with my hands tied behind my back and shot by six men with machine guns.

By the time we dug our foxholes in Kapoeta, things had totally changed for me as a soldier. In Koi River, I had been given certain freedoms, thanks to my family connections to Mabior Kuir Maketh. I had been allowed to visit the Dimma refugee camp pretty much whenever I pleased and we kept well out of harm's way. But now I was in the theatre of war and fully accountable to the SPLA and its hierarchy.

Kapoeta was being run at the time by a senior Dinka commander who had a reputation as a fearsome warrior: one of those guys our wartime songs warned about. He ordered counter-attacks on the local Toposa bandits and on one occasion, many local tribesmen were slaughtered.

Our commando unit was no longer in the business of running guns, storing munitions or singing war songs for visiting dignitaries. Like everyone else, we spent the days just passing time and mentally preparing to be attacked at any moment. I had been assigned to ride along with my old singing friend, Napoleon, who'd been tasked with driving the local ambulance in service of Kapoeta Hospital's respected medico, Dr Achol. At least it gave us something to take our minds away from the steadily mounting tension.

Although the SPLA had driven the Arab fighters out of Kapoeta a couple of years earlier, now that we had been forced to abandon our bases in Ethiopia, the Sudanese government forces sensed weakness and, word had it, they were preparing to re-take Kapoeta. It was a daunting, depressing thought. And who knew whose side the Toposa would take when the shooting started?

The stress of it all played tricks on my mind. One night I dreamed I was in a room with some other soldiers when I heard the shriek of an approaching jet.

'It's a bomber!' I shouted.

Everybody grabbed their guns and ran outside with me. I stopped for a second to try to sense which direction the plane was coming from. I leaped over a fence, sprinted across the dreamscape and dived into a foxhole. I made it with a split second to spare before immense tremors caused by one hundred Arab bombs wiped Kapoeta off the map.

'Argh!' I jolted awake with my heart pounding against my ribs.

At about eleven o'clock the next morning, that nightmare came true. I don't want to say I had a premonition – only that the Arab air attack followed the exact script as my dream. The sound of a jet engine scraped across the sky, scattering us like startled animals as we scrambled for our foxholes. After the jet tore past, I heard the whistle of air rushing by the bombs' stabiliser fins followed by a series of deafening blasts and bone-jarring concussions. There was no fighting back against jet bombers – all I could do was cling to the wall of my foxhole and pray the next bomb didn't land on top of me.

The Arab pilots were wickedly smart; they'd drop a line of bombs along one trajectory then loop around and make another run, this time crossing the original path of devastation at right angles. The next two passes would intersect the target area diagonally so that, from above, Kapoeta would have resembled a giant human dartboard that had been strafed along eight different axes.

People who understood this knew that if a bomb fell near them they should just stay put until it was all over. Unfortunately a lot of people didn't know that and ran away from bombed areas only to be hit during the jet's second, third or fourth pass. The attack was carried out with devastatingly surgical precision and it seemed to go on forever.

Only when I was sure the plane was gone for good did I crawl out of my foxhole and run to the part of the town that had been worst hit. I found Napoleon there picking up casualties so I jumped into the Toyota LandCruiser that served as our ambulance and we started transporting the wounded soldiers and civilians to Kapoeta's little hospital.

The scene was horrific. People were missing large chunks of themselves and several had their arms or legs blown off. The shrapnel tore gaping, gory holes in people and the sight of the dead was almost too terrible to behold. One soldier – a relative of my cousin Ruben – suffered a direct hit from a bomb. The thing detonated on his head and left almost nothing of him behind. We identified him by his belt.

There were thirty-five casualties that day, five who died and many who were maimed for life. The air was filled with screaming, shouting and weeping but I tried to keep one ear out for the distant growl of a jet engine. We just knew they were coming back.

The bombing continued for months but nothing was as bad as that first air raid. Everyone in Kapoeta – the refugees, the civilians and the SPLA – had found some sort of hole they could take cover in when the jets returned with their litter of bombs. The casualties were never as great as they'd been on day one but the mental suffering that comes with being hunted from the air was always the same.

In the middle of this chaos, in early 1992, I was finally reunited with my mum and my younger siblings Garang and Akeer, who had been stranded in tribal lands further to the north. It was the first time I had seen them in six years.

Mum told me my other brother Deng had also joined the Red Army but the rest of them had remained in our village of Awulian until 1990 when they became hemmed in between two wars: the north and south Sudanese conflict and a bitter fight that had erupted between Dinka and Nuer. One day the Nuer attacked the village and embarked on a killing spree. My beloved grandmother Duop was among those slaughtered.

Grandma had become blind in her old age and was caring for one of her infant grandchildren inside her hut when the Nuer attacked without warning. Unable to run away, Grandma and the baby were burned alive after the Nuer set fire to the dry, grassy walls of her humble home. The news tore my heart out. I wept nonstop, remembering innocent days with her at Awulian. There was no one like Grandma – she was the one who always looked out for us, the one who comforted us the most and who snuck extra food or milk to us as a treat when we'd been good. Who could kill someone so old, so blind and so full of love? My fury burned white hot.

Mum had escaped with the two youngest ones and while she was on the run she somehow got word that Aguil, Yar and I had ended up in Kapoeta and decided to risk travelling there. It was a dicey decision; the Arab pilots controlled us from the air while the government marshalled troops, tanks and artillery on the ground.

The Arabs knew there were a lot of innocent South Sudanese sheltering in Kapoeta. They also knew the SPLA's strength was depleted after we were driven out of Ethiopia.

It was just a matter of time before they launched an assault to wipe us all out.

After just a few blessed days reconnecting with my mother and siblings, I had to leave Kapoeta with the commandos. We were to resume running guns – this time on the Ugandan border about seventy kilometres to the south. Mabior Maketh had overseen the construction of a new secret arms base there and called it Lotuke. Not long after we arrived in Lotuke we heard rumours that an Arab ground assault on Kapoeta was imminent. I cried for my mum and siblings and prayed for their souls.

A couple of days later we heard the distant sound of bomber sorties and artillery pounding Kapoeta as the attack began. When the government's ground forces advanced, their ranks were swelled by the mercurial Toposa militia.

Later we received reports about captured SPLA rebels and innocent civilians being rounded up and gunned down by the allied Arab–Toposa fighters. Many of the dead had been targeted simply because they weren't Toposa and they were in the wrong territory. It was with a mixture of shock, grief, shame and dread that I was left to ponder whether my family were among those who'd been slaughtered and if the bullets I'd traded for meat and milk were the ones that took their lives. A few weeks later the crushing weight of worry lifted just a little when we finally got word that all of my family had managed to escape from Kapoeta just before it fell.

'Thank you, God,' I whispered. I started to have doubts, however, about whether He would spare me so I could see them again.

7

WAR CHILD

The new base at Lotuke was bigger than our old jungle camp at Koi River. Our ranks of a few hundred were mostly filled with child soldiers but despite our numbers we were in even more danger than we had been in while running guns in Ethiopia. Lotuke had been built on top of a small hill in tribal lands belonging to the Didinga people, who just happened to foster a deep hatred of the Dinka and the SPLA. As we brought arms and uniforms across the border from allies in Uganda, the Didinga saw us as bringing the war to their doorstep. They attacked us constantly.

By that stage just about every ethnic group in Sudan's south was well armed, mostly with stolen guns that had once belonged to the SPLA. Many had been trained like I had in Ethiopia and had simply returned to their tribe with a nice new AK-47, ready to defend their traditional lands. Although the civil war was cast as a battle between north and south, in truth we faced a brand-new enemy and a brand-new war almost everywhere we turned. When the Didinga heard Kapoeta had fallen to the Arabs, they launched a series of guerrilla attacks on our position at Lotuke in which several boy soldiers lost their lives.

Not all Didinga recruits who'd been trained by the SPLA had deserted and run back home. At least, not straightaway. One of the senior SPLA officers in our commando guard was a Didinga man who had served alongside us for years. After the fall of Kapoeta, however, he must have seen the writing on the wall and one night he fled Lotuke without warning and headed to the nearby mountain villages of his tribe.

It was a serious blow and, in a bid to calm tensions, Mabior sent four of our men up the mountain to try to reach a peace deal with the Didinga. The diplomacy was to be handled by one of our Dinka officers and the muscle was provided by a beast of a man we called Silah, which is Arabic for 'gun'.

A hulking tribesman from the Nuba Mountains, Silah was the only soldier I can honestly say was a match for the great white commando Arnold Schwarzenegger. Silah made an AK-47 look like a popgun when he cradled it in his massive arms. Instead, he usually carried a large, heavy machine gun called an MG 42, just like the one Arnold used in *Commando*. On this day, however, Silah took a lighter Kalashnikov because the delegation had a long, steep hike ahead of them.

After scaling the jungle-covered slopes for hours the four soldiers reached the Didinga village in the late afternoon.

Our Dinka officer sat down with the tribal chief and tried to reason him into agreeing to a ceasefire: 'Why do you shoot at us? What have we done wrong? OK, we're here in your land but there's a war. We give you food and we don't try to hurt you. We're getting weapons from Uganda to fight for our country – for all of us.'

The talks had barely gotten underway when the high-ranking SPLA deserter suddenly appeared among the Didinga. Sensing trouble, Silah stood up and, without hesitation, opened fire on the officer. Whether it was a pre-emptive strike or a summary punishment for his desertion, it triggered a hurricane of bullets. We heard it all back in Lotuke: the fatal first shot, followed by scores of chattering Kalashnikovs. We got the full story later that night after the Dinka officer made it down the mountainside and into camp. He said Silah and the others had been shot and were most likely dead, along with numerous Didinga.

It was a big blow to our morale – Silah and the others had been among our toughest fighters and losing them made us feel all the more vulnerable. The next morning, however, we were shocked when Silah dragged himself back into Lotuke. He'd taken a couple of bullets in the belly but had managed to find cover and stay hidden on the mountainside overnight before crawling back down through thick jungle and across treacherous mountain creeks when dawn broke.

The poor man was so sweaty, so tired and covered in so much dried blood it was hard to make out his uniform. It had been a huge effort to come back down that mountain and it was only because of his massive size that he was able to keep going. It was all for nothing though. Silah died a few hours later.

After that, the Didinga attacked us every chance they got. The steep, hilly borderlands were covered with dense vegetation, and dissected by rivulets and streams that gave them plenty of places to hide. All they had to do was surround the base and lie in wait. Like the Toposa, the Didinga were adept at ambushing us when we needed to have a shit. Sometimes they'd kill boys with rocks or clubs to the head and other times they'd just shoot us.

It was a quiet, sunny afternoon when I decided to go to the toilet near a creek about a hundred and fifty metres down the hill from our base. There hadn't been any Didinga attacks all week so, while I was still cautious, I didn't feel like my number was up.

'I'm going for a shit, guys,' I said as I set off. 'Watch my back, OK?'

I didn't take my gun with me because I felt my comrades had me pretty well covered from their foxholes. The grass along the creek was a safe, waist-high length so I settled onto my haunches behind a tree to do my business. All the while I could see my guys up on the hill walking around and chatting to each other. As soon as I finished I got onto one knee, pulled my pants up and stood upright. Big mistake. The air whizzed with bullets that made strange zipping noises as they split the grass and buried into the soft earth around me.

Instead of diving onto my belly and staying low in the grass like I'd been drilled to in basic training, my panicked

mind defaulted to another well-practised manoeuvre –
I bolted up the hill for my life, zig-zagging all the way as
more bullets tore past me and thudded into the ground.
My guys screamed at me, 'Get down! GET DOWN!' but
I just kept bobbing and weaving up the hillside. In the next
moment the rebels opened fire towards the creek and the
source of the gunshots. That's when it occurred to me why
they were screaming at me to hit the ground: I was caught
in a crossfire.

Miraculously I made it back to base without so much as
a scratch. I dived for my gun and went to join the firefight
but by the time I'd leaped into a foxhole and took aim
it was all over. We quickly worked out it was just a few
Didinga guys taking potshots and not an all-out attack.
I also came in for some serious ribbing for my hillside
dance moves.

That night I lay awake thinking about a friendly enough
Didinga boy I'd gotten to know in the Red Army camp.
His name was Black and he was one of the many boys who
escaped with a gun and ran back home. Maybe Black was
one of the people who'd tried to blow my head off down
at the creek that afternoon. I'll never know and it didn't
really matter. I was just happy to still be above ground
and breathing. While it had been a harrowing experience
I clung half-heartedly to the idea that whatever doesn't kill
you makes you stronger.

—

I had grown used to death. That's not to say I was numb to it; there's a hurt you feel, especially when it's someone you know, and even when people are injured, it scars you. I'd had to face those potent emotions from an early age – ever since I'd seen the fallen Mandari warrior with an arrow in his chest, and the sunken corpse that had been dumped at the Juba garbage tip. As more bodies piled up in my mind, however, they started to have an effect on me.

I had always been a quick-tempered little kid but my time in the Red Army had turned me into a perpetually angry, sullen and volatile teenager. A casual observer could have been forgiven for thinking I was becoming seriously unhinged. By 1993 I didn't care about myself any more. I had no dreams or ambitions beyond the next five minutes and I had nothing to lose – not a good frame of mind for a young person with a gun to be in.

One day I travelled with some other boy soldiers to a nearby refugee camp where a market was in full swing. It was a typical African get-together with great crowds of people from different tribes dancing in groups on a large field. I'd left my AK-47 back at the base because the market was considered a safe environment where ninety per cent of the people were civilian and everyone was there to have fun. Instead, I packed my pistol on my hip and covered it over with my untucked camouflage shirt.

There was lots going on at the refugee camp beyond just dancing. People had set up stalls to sell knick-knacks, food, spices and even some homemade beer. I swallowed some mouthfuls of the home-brew and wandered, tipsy, around the markets in the heat of the afternoon.

My friends and I were threading through the thick crowds, watching the different tribes perform their dances when a random guy either bumped into me or said something that I can't even remember. Whatever the perceived insult was, I reacted by calmly pulling out my pistol, cocking it and shoving it into his face. I was about to pull the trigger when my friends realised what was happening.

'No, no, no, no, no, Ayik!' they pleaded. 'What are you doing? Don't do it! Don't shoot him!'

Their startled reaction snapped me out of whatever killer trance I was in and I quickly cooled and re-holstered my weapon. A high-ranking SPLA officer who'd come to watch the dancers saw what I had done. His bodyguards arrested me on the spot, took my pistol off me and locked me up overnight in an old-fashioned bush prison made of thorns. When I was released the next morning they gave me my gun back.

'Hey,' the officer said as he handed the pistol over, 'why did you behave like that?'

I mumbled something small-minded about how the stranger had pissed me off but the fact was I didn't really understand why I had gone from watching dancers to being on the verge of killing a man in cold blood. It wasn't the first or last time I'd pull a gun on an innocent person in a misguided teenage show of force. To me, the gun truly had become everything. It was the same for a lot of boy soldiers.

There were many occasions when Red Army recruits of only twelve, thirteen and fourteen shot people dead just to settle a score or because they'd been bullied or belittled. Often the victim was a fellow soldier or a superior, as was the case with the murder–suicide in Raad. One day I came close to doing the same thing myself.

I was one of five bodyguards at Lotuke who was assigned to live in the same house with my Aunty Dew and Mabior Maketh. The highest-ranking bodyguard was a man in his thirties named Mabek. Aside from providing security we took turns doing household chores including cleaning Aunty Dew and Mabior's guns – two or three AK-47s, hunting rifles and a few pistols – washing their clothes and bedding, cooking, fixing fences and maintaining the foxholes.

One morning it was my turn to cook for the other bodyguards, which meant standing up for hours pounding maize with a giant mortar and pestle in order to make asida, which is similar to porridge but thicker and used to dunk into stews. I was so weak from severe dysentery, however, that I could barely move let alone cook. It was not unusual for soldiers to fall ill with malaria or suffer horrendous bouts of dysentery from any number of viruses, bacteria and parasites that made their home in the jungle. Mabek had gone across the border to Uganda to pick up a shipment of guns and when he returned he was very displeased that there was nothing to eat.

'Who was supposed to cook today?' Mabek asked.

'Ayik was,' one of the commandos responded, 'but he's very unwell.'

Mabek ordered three child soldiers to drag me outside into the sun and discipline me in the SPLA fashion. It was basically a re-run of the torture that was inflicted on me in the Red Army camp in Ethiopia. The boys forced me to roll back and forth across the baking hot ground, run up and down hills until I almost fainted, perform squat jumps thirty metres this way then thirty metres back, and stand on one foot for as long as I was told. Whenever my other foot touched the ground they whipped me. The only thing missing was Anyang and his chilli powder.

After several long, agonising hours of suffering I reached my breaking point. A switch in my brain flipped onto the 'kill' setting. With no control over my actions, I broke away from the child soldiers and charged towards my room where I knew my trusty Kalashnikov was loaded and waiting. Once I had it, I would hunt Mabek down and shoot him in the head.

As I reached my room, however, Mabek appeared in the doorway and tackled me to the ground. A second later the child soldiers landed on top of me too. Because he instinctively knew what I was capable of, Mabek had wisely waited in my room in case I tried to exact revenge. The foresight saved his life that day and while the vain bid to assassinate Mabek brought the torture session to an end, the episode only pushed my latent rage dangerously into the red.

Had I been deployed to the front lines of the war I likely would have had an outlet for all the hate and anger; I would have fought, shot and killed, like so many other child soldiers had done. But my family connections meant I was always up the back and on the borders – not out of harm's way, but definitely removed from wholesale daily slaughter. As a result, little things could set me off, be it a 'wrong' look from a stranger at a market, a beating at the behest of a superior or being shot at by tribal militia.

We couldn't drive our trucks anywhere without being ambushed, usually by little groups of three to five tribesmen with a few AK-47s and maybe a rocket-propelled grenade or two. But since we were gun-runners our firepower was superior to small-time local militia. We would return their potshots with great barrages of machine-gun fire and volleys of grenades that shredded pockets of jungle.

Because we were always firing on the move it was impossible to know whether or not any of our rounds had found their mark. These running gunfights might only last two or three minutes before the bush fell silent again and we'd be on our way. While I never got to confront the enemy face-to-face, I fired hundreds of rounds at where I thought they were hiding. I may have injured or killed people during those exchanges but I will never know, which is definitely for the best.

I had settled on a personal code when it came to the morality of killing in war. I had no problem shooting at someone who was shooting at me but there were things I promised myself I would never do. I knew soldiers who had 'finished off' injured enemy fighters with a pistol shot to the head rather than take them prisoner. To me that was murder. As soon as someone was unarmed and not firing at me I considered them no longer a threat. I believed we were honour-bound to take them captive.

I swore I would never kill elderly people, women, babies or young children either. My stance was shaped by the evil that befell my grandmother at the hands of the Nuer and I knew if I were involved in anything like that it would haunt me to the point I could no longer live with myself. There was one exception in my rules of engagement – plenty of little kids ran around Sudan with AK-47s and hand grenades, and if one pulled a gun on me I knew I would have no choice but to shoot them first. Kill or be killed. I hated the war.

A kid I never thought I'd try to kill, however, was me. That changed on the day I grabbed hold of an anti-tank grenade and threatened to blow myself and everybody around me to smithereens. I was on a mission somewhere outside of Lotuke with a group of SPLA and boy soldiers. We stopped in a small town where the local tribesmen were trading milk, home-brew, chickens, goats, sorghum and maize.

Once again, the trouble started after I drank some of the locally made beer. It was rare for me to consume alcohol so it didn't take much to make me drunk. I was sitting under a tree having a slurred conversation with another kid about some subject I can't recall when a big-mouthed guy rudely interrupted me. I was so enraged I walked over to one of the trucks and picked up an anti-tank grenade. The Russian-built device was about a foot long and packed with enough explosives to wipe out every living thing within a ten-metre radius.

I returned to the tree where a lot of guys were still sitting around – some were even sleeping. These were people I knew and liked but none of that mattered; I'd had enough of the world and was ready to put an end to it for all of us. When they saw what I was holding and read the expression on my face I had everybody's full attention.

'Please, Ayik,' I heard a quavering voice say. 'Put the grenade down. You will kill yourself and everyone else here.'

Yes, that was the plan.

'Please, Ayik, please! Think about what you're doing. Everybody here will die. We want to live.'

After a few minutes all the pleading and begging started to penetrate my drunken, war-addled brain. I reassessed the need for a mass-murder–suicide and decided to let everyone live after all. I put the monster grenade down and fell asleep under the tree.

Episodes like that made me realise that when things didn't kill me they didn't just make me stronger. They made me angrier, more confused and more dangerous as well.

—

The hot, dirty winds of war had scattered my family throughout southern Sudan. Most of the time I had no idea where any of them were but even though hundreds upon thousands of civilians had been slaughtered in the conflict already, I refused to believe my own loved ones were among the dead. 'If I am alive then they probably are too,' remained my mantra.

Then in mid-1993 Aunty Dew found out my mum was living in Nimule, a ramshackle town on the Sudan–Uganda border a few days' drive from our base at Lotuke.

'Would you like to go and see her?' Aunty Dew asked.

Although getting there would mean a journey through hostile tribal land, I didn't need to be asked twice. A few days after receiving the good news, we rumbled out of Lotuke in a small convoy of several trucks and a few Toyota LandCruisers fitted with heavy machine guns. As usual, we came under small-arms fire as we snaked through the hills and jungle villages and, as usual, we returned the favour in spades until we finally arrived in Nimule unscathed a day or two later.

I was overjoyed to see Mum again but she had her hands full caring for Aguil's two young sons Dut and Dhieu. Aguil's husband was an SPLA captain who was away fighting in the war. My big sister had powerful connections of her own in the upper levels of the SPLA and was apparently somewhere on the border of Kenya and Sudan investigating how to get all of her loved ones out of our haemorrhaging homeland. Yar, Garang, Deng and Akeer were apparently safe too, but we weren't sure exactly where.

When the rest of the commando unit returned to Lotuke a few days later I was allowed to stay behind in Nimule and help Mum take care of my nephews until Aguil returned.

Rebel life was a lot quieter in Nimule. I didn't once get

shot at while having a shit, nor was I ambushed, whipped or forced to stand on one foot for an hour. Reconnecting with Mum was bittersweet; while it was wonderful to be with her again, a lot of our conversations revolved around all of the people in our family who were now dead.

After a few months of relative calm in Nimule, the full horror of the war came crashing back in. Aunty Dew sent word that Arab bombers had struck Lotuke and that one of Mabior's bodyguards, my good friend John Lokoro, had been killed. I was devastated and I wept bitterly for him. Although he was a good deal older than me, John had been like a brother. He had taken me under his wing from day one at Koi River and lately, whenever he accompanied Mabior across the border into Uganda he had taken to bringing me gifts like a new shirt or a pair of shoes. During my time at Lotuke I had shared a room with John and three other guys – the same room the Arabs had bombed, killing my dear friend instantly. Had I been with him instead of at Nimule with Mum, I might have been blown to pieces, too.

Apparently the Didinga militia had tipped the Arabs off about the location of the base. It was a grim signal that government forces were gaining momentum in the south and pushing us out of our strongholds. First Kapoeta fell, followed by many small towns and villages in the surrounding region. Now that Lotuke was under attack we worried that Nimule would be next. Indeed word had reached us that some villages nearby had already been hit.

Finally, as the war closed in around us, Mum received a message from Aguil: she had managed to organise passage for us to travel to Nairobi in Kenya, another of Sudan's friendly southern neighbours. Apparently I was among a group of young people who would be going to school there to become future leaders of a free and independent South Sudan. Or so the story went – in my mind it was just an invitation to run from the war and not look back.

Only very senior SPLA commanders and their aides could carry weapons across the border into Uganda or Kenya, and even then only with permission of the host government. If a lowly boy soldier like me wanted to enter Kenya then he had to do so unarmed. That was just fine by me. Having once coveted and even worshipped the AK-47, I had grown sick of carrying a gun everywhere I went. I was glad to hand the thing in at the SPLA arms depot at Nimule.

Mum and I gathered up Aguil's boys and clambered onto the back of one of the three trucks that were due to drive us in convoy more than four hundred kilometres to Lokichogio, a town just across the border in northern Kenya. The women and children were seated in the middle of the trucks while the soldiers sat on both sides and at the back, ready to leap down and fight in case of an attack.

Aguil had managed to piggyback our escape onto that of the wife and children of a rebel general named Kuol Manyang Juuk. He had a dark reputation and most rebel soldiers were scared of him. Now that I was in a convoy carrying his family to safety and under the protection of his bodyguards, I thought he was fantastic.

As the trucks loaded with human cargo set off, we were flanked by heavily armed soldiers in jeeps and LandCruisers fitted with machine guns. I was seated on the tailgate of the last truck, facing backwards with my feet dangling in the air and watching the jeep behind us follow in our tyre tracks. A cloud of dust billowed up from the dirt road and as I wiped my face with my sleeve I heard the familiar rattle of AK-47s being fired at us and bullets pinging into the vehicles.

Some soldiers leaped off the trucks before they'd even stopped, took up positions and returned fire. Instinctively I jumped off, too, dismayed I'd handed in my gun less than an hour earlier. All I could do was take cover underneath the truck and keep an eye out to see if any of our guys got killed or injured; then I'd be able to take his weapon and join the fight.

Being unarmed in a firefight was a terrible feeling. I knew that if the people shooting at us managed to overwhelm us we would all be killed; we'd likely be tied up and shot one by one. Dying like that was my greatest fear. As I cowered under the grime-covered belly of the truck I prayed to God that if one of our guys was killed I'd be able to get his gun and ammo so I could die fighting – not shot in the back of the head like my beloved brother Aleer. Meanwhile, Mum, the boys and the other civilians pressed themselves flat against the floor of the lorries. In between the bursts of gunfire I could hear them praying, too.

After three or four minutes, the incoming fire ceased and our soldiers screamed, 'Is everyone OK? Is everyone OK?' Amazingly, no one died in the ambush, although several people were injured. Mum had a close shave; the soldier who'd been sitting next to her had his gun struck by an incoming round, which caused it to jam.

Everyone was on edge for the rest of the journey to Kenya but it seemed God had heard all our prayers. We managed to cross the border the following night without anyone else trying to kill us.

When I breached the invisible line that separated Kenya from Sudan the war suddenly ended for me. For more than two years I had managed to duck and weave through the turmoil and endless peril and emerge without a single injury. At least, none that you could see.

8

INTO AFRICA

It was dark when we pulled up outside a hotel in Lokichogio and I was stunned by the amount of light that flooded the night around it. There were lights inside and outside the hotel itself and there were even lights on the street. Lokichogio was the most civilised place I had seen. Perhaps because I was safe for the first time in years, I felt strangely good about myself, so much so that I started flirting with General Kuol Manyang's daughter, a beautiful young woman named Atong Kuol.

'I love you,' I told Atong, trying to act as cool as possible. (In Dinka, there is no distinction between 'like' and 'love'.) 'Yeah, I love you and I want you to be my wife.'

The great romance ended a few minutes later when we were hurriedly transferred onto a bus to continue our journey south to the capital because our SPLA trucks weren't registered to drive in Kenya. The further along the road to Nairobi we travelled, the better Kenya seemed to get. There were lots of buildings, lots of people and lots of cars driving along neat, orderly streets that were illuminated by rows of overheard lights. But the most striking thing I noticed about Kenya was the obvious state of overall calm; the people looked happy and no one was carrying a gun.

We arrived in Nairobi exhausted at about 3 am. The bus pulled up outside a unit rented by Aguil in the suburb of Zimmerman and when I walked in, I was delighted to find all my brothers and sisters there, too.

The unit seemed to shrink in the daylight. It was a two-bedroom affair with a tiny kitchen and one small sitting room. Although there was no electricity, the kitchen was fitted with a small gas cooker. I noticed something else that made the unit feel more cramped and claustrophobic; the metal front door had bars across the top half and a glass panel on the inside. All the other windows had bars on the outside, too. The place could easily have doubled as a prison.

To support the family, Aguil relied on a trickle of sponsorships from a number of charity groups including the Red Cross and the UNHCR, and individuals in powerful positions. Even so, ours was by far the poorest family in Zimmerman. As I decompressed from the war over the following months I got to know a few other Sudanese families who lived in the same suburb. Because of the language barrier, however, I found it hard to communicate with the locals. I hardly knew a word of English or Swahili beyond my name, 'hello', 'yes' and 'no' – but it didn't stop me from leaving the house and roaming the streets. Over time I got to know a few Kenyans, too, including a wonderful guy named George. He was a photographer and I organised for quite a few of the local Sudanese to have family portraits taken by him.

As I explored the streets of Zimmerman I started to broaden my understanding of the world beyond my war-torn homeland. One day I walked past a shop that was selling televisions that were stacked on top of each other in the front window. I noticed every set was showing the same images at the same time and that's when the penny dropped: TV wasn't a magical view into another world! It was just a device that broadcast moving photographs taken with a different kind of camera.

George owned a television and I spent a lot of time at his place watching Bollywood movies from India. I also became familiar with a show called *Neighbours*, which was about beautiful young white people who walked around nice houses talking to each other all day. I couldn't understand a word of what they were saying and I couldn't figure out if the white people lived in Kenya or not but it was enjoyable to watch all the same.

I may have struggled with English and Swahili but there was one universal language I was fluent in: football (in Australia: soccer). I had played the round-ball game with my friends in the commando guard, and I'd become pretty good at it. There was a soccer field around the corner from our unit in Zimmerman and I often ended up there, kicking a ball with my newfound Sudanese friends. One evening I learned a hard lesson that not all Kenyans were as cool and as welcoming as my friend George.

We were playing soccer about 6 pm when a gang of Kenyan teenagers descended on the park and started in on us. They jeered us, threatened us and eventually snatched our ball and booted it away down the street. Enraged by the bullying, I picked up some rocks and started pelting the Kenyan thugs. Fighting with stones is common among African boys, but this skirmish quickly got out of hand. We outnumbered our tormentors and soon had them on the run under a hail of rocks.

Emboldened, we gave chase and as I drew closer to one of the Kenyan kids I picked up a brick and hurled it, striking him in the back of the head. He fell hard, face-first onto the ground and didn't move. In a panic we ran back to the park, grabbed our stuff and bolted home.

That night I hardly slept, haunted by the thought that the bully I'd bricked might be dead. I had managed to fight in and survive a war without knowingly killing a soul and now, in the first few months of civilian life, I could have blood on my hands over nothing more than a little bullying and a stolen soccer ball. As soon as the sun came up, I ran back to the park and was greatly relieved to find no corpse on the ground and no police investigating a murder.

Although life in Kenya was tranquil compared to Sudan, veins of hatred and violence still ran deep through the community. I was out walking one morning when I saw a mob chasing after a man. I followed to see what the commotion was about when they cornered him and started chanting 'Mwizi! Mwizi! Mwizi!' ('Thief! Thief! Thief!') He was a handsome young guy in his twenties but he had a look of sheer terror in his eyes.

I was horrified when the crowd started throwing large rocks at him and he quickly fell to the ground. Before I knew what was happening, a car tyre had been hung around his neck, filled with petrol and set alight. I couldn't watch as the poor guy turned to smoke right there on the street. I don't know what he was supposed to have stolen but it couldn't have been worth that.

Theft was considered a most heinous crime in Kenya – apparently far worse than burning people alive. If you stole something in Kenya, the only way you'd be safe was if you ran to the police for protection. The terrifying thing is there appeared to be no legal process for testing such allegations, it was a matter of, 'He stole my watch. Let's burn him!' A couple of months later the same thing almost happened to me.

I was standing in the aisle of a crowded bus as it wound through the streets of Zimmerman when an old lady started yelling in Swahili, 'Mwizi! Mwizi!' I looked around the bus to see who the poor 'thief' was, but now the old lady was shouting, 'Nyeusi! Nyeusi!' ('Black! Black!') Then I realised she was pointing at me.

In Ethiopia and Kenya – where a lot of people had lighter shades of skin – I learned people with very dark skin like mine were looked upon with disgust and contempt. Since

I hadn't stolen anything from the angry old lady, I assumed she had taken a dislike to my pigment and was anxious to see me set on fire.

'Black thief! Black thief!' she kept shrieking as the bus lumbered along. Other passengers were looking at me, too. None of them were smiling.

'Black thief! Black thief!'

'What! Me?' I exploded at the old lady, wild-eyed and incredulous. 'Me not mwizi! I've got my own money!'

I started pulling loose coins and my bus ticket from my pockets to back up my poor attempts at Swahili. I'd had to pay for the ticket to get on the bus in the first place so at least the driver knew I had my own means.

'This is my money. MY MONEY!' I bellowed, tapping it to my chest. 'I don't steal.'

My outrage at being accused was plain for all to see and it was enough to defuse the woman's attack; she shut her mouth and the other passengers left me alone.

I couldn't help thinking how that day might easily have been my last. It was lucky I'd been on a bus; I could see how an episode like that might escalate had it taken place out on the street. As soon as you tried to get away from the false accuser, people would instinctively give chase and before you knew it you'd be turned into smoke.

—

Aguil had been deadly serious. I *was* going to attend school in Kenya, although whether I emerged from the experience as one of Sudan's new generation of leaders remained to be seen. I had been enrolled at a boarding school for well-to-do people in Kapenguria, a town in a farming region over four hundred kilometres north-west of Nairobi. Using her powerful political connections, Aguil had also arranged for me to stay in a fourteen-bedroom mansion with members of SPLA leader Dr John Garang's extended family for the first few months of the school year. By the time a bed became available for me in the boarding school dormitory, however, I already hated the place.

Already a stranger in a strange land, I felt like an even bigger freak in Kapenguria – mainly because I was so far behind everybody else academically. It was obvious to all and it made me cringe with embarrassment. My fellow students were becoming fluent in English and speaking it in that precise, polished way so many Africans do – 'Good day to you, sir. How are you feeling? May I interest you in a glass of water?' I was still struggling with single words such as 'hello', 'please', 'thank you' and 'goodbye'.

Whenever the teacher asked questions of the class, twenty eager hands shot into the air while mine remained jammed in the pockets of my shorts as I glowered from the back row, a tactical vantage point from which I could see anyone approaching. Now and then I'd hear the word 'nyeusi' murmured in my vicinity. Still, I managed to make a few friends, including a Kenyan boy named Oscar. He lived in a house about two hundred metres from the school with his mother, younger brother and younger sister. On the weekends he'd invite me over for lunch and dinner.

If you were observing from the outside, my life would have appeared pretty good compared to most South Sudanese at that point in history. I was attending an excellent school, I had food, friends, people cared about me and I wasn't being shot at. Strangely, the latter was part of the problem. I knew who I *really* was: Daniel Ayik Chut Deng, Red Army soldier and seasoned rebel fighter. I had no business going to school! I was a tribesman whose future lay in farming cattle, if only we could win the civil war first. The more time I spent failing at school, the more I wanted to return to Sudan, get my gun back and start fighting the Arabs.

One day I asked Oscar if there was any way he could help me get a bus ticket to return to my family in Nairobi. He went home that day and asked his mum to help me. She bought me a ticket straightaway and a few days later I was on a bus back to the capital. When I walked through the steel-barred door of Aguil's apartment in Zimmerman she was at first shocked to see me. Then she was angry.

'What are you doing here?' she demanded. 'Why aren't you in school?'

'Because I hate it,' I fired back. 'I don't belong there.'

Aguil was aghast that I had squandered the opportunity she'd arranged for my benefit. But I was just as angry at her.

'Listen, Aguil, you brought me here to Kenya so now I want you to give me some money so I can go back home and fight,' I said.

'That's not going to happen,' she scoffed.

Begrudgingly, she let me stay in the unit. After a while,

the pull of the war grew so strong and I felt so useless in Kenya that I told Aguil I was going to leave the next day.

'OK,' she said. 'Whatever. Fine.'

When I woke the next morning I sensed something was different. As I brushed the last wisps of sleep from my face and prepared to get up I was struck by how quiet the place was. You could have heard a pin drop in the apartment, which was strange because the little ones always had their voices set on the highest volume.

I looked in the other rooms and was surprised to find no one else was at home. Weird! I went to open the front door so I could look for my family outside but, oddly, it wouldn't budge. I tried the handle again but the damned thing seemed to be locked. I peered through the glass pane of the door and that's when I saw the large padlock clamped on a bolt on the outside. I'd been locked in! Aguil had imprisoned me.

A quick look around confirmed there was no escape – all of the windows were protected by strong steel bars that were fitted onto the outside of the glass. I flew into a rage. I picked up a metal bar that we kept in the unit and smashed all of the windows and tried to crash through the front door. As I screamed, cried and careened about the unit, neighbours came out of their homes to see what was happening but nobody tried to help me get out. After all, we were in Africa; they probably thought I'd wronged my family and was being punished deservedly.

When Aguil returned later that afternoon she was confronted by the sight of a trashed apartment, shattered windows and an angry brother. Instead of letting me out, she called the police. I was arrested, handcuffed, taken to a police station in Zimmerman and locked in a cell overnight.

Aguil had asked that I be charged with destroying property and I had to face court the next day. The following afternoon I was released on the condition that Mum and my brother Deng sign a document saying they would take responsibility if I committed any other offences. Two days later I scrounged together enough money from friends to buy a bus ticket out of Nairobi.

The journey took me to Dadaab, a small town in the Kenyan desert about five hundred kilometres north-east of Nairobi. At that time, a lot of people were travelling there in the belief the territory was actually inside Somalia. I thought it was, too, and I figured by going to Somalia I would somehow find an easier passage back to Sudan, even though it was in the opposite direction.

When the doors of the bus opened in Dadaab I truly believed I *was* in Somalia. All of the police were Somali, as were the soldiers and civilians. I was taken aside by police officers who wanted to know who I was, where I was going and why I didn't have a visa considering I was a Sudanese man who appeared to be crossing Kenya on his way to Somalia. I told them I was a refugee but they ruled that I was in the region illegally and told me I was going to be locked up.

The prison at Dadaab was a step up in security from the thorny cages I'd learned to escape from in Sudan. It had solid walls, locking doors and it was ringed by a high fence topped with barbed wire. In spite of that, and the fact I was locked inside a large enclosure with forty or fifty other potentially dangerous inmates, I wasn't frightened. As far as everyone else was concerned I was a primitive being. I had no real grip on Swahili and I couldn't speak a word of Somali so I simply kept to myself while everyone else ignored me.

About two months later I was released and taken to Ifo Refugee Camp, a bustling UN facility about two kilometres along a dusty road from Dadaab. Once again I could have been forgiven for thinking I was in Somalia. Most of the women wore the hijab, most of the men wore Islamic macawis that looked like a sarong and shawl, and they all bowed to Mecca to pray five times a day.

For the second time in my life UN officials asked me my name, where I was from and my date of birth. At that point, by their earlier reckoning at Dimma, I was eighteen years old. I couldn't rightly tell them my true purpose for being there – that I was plotting to somehow get back to the war in Sudan – otherwise I would have been sent back to prison in Dadaab. Instead, I told them I was a refugee.

My newfound status ensured I received UN rations to eat and it also meant I was automatically placed on a register of people eligible for resettlement overseas. Thousands of people at Ifo struggled through each day in the hope they'd eventually be welcomed into the bosom of the West and given a new life abroad. Not me – I was still intent on fighting.

I was sent to live in the Sudanese section of the refugee camp where, incredibly, I ran into my long-lost best friend, Daniel Deng Manyok. He'd managed to escape from Sudan, too, but we didn't dare swap our war stories. Instead we hung out together and played soccer with the other refugees.

Unsurprisingly, there's not much to do in a refugee camp. The days melt into one another and people tend to just sit around and think. After six months in Ifo my most memorable achievements were learning how to play chess and making a pair of camel-skin shoes.

Some Somalians had killed a camel and sold it to the refugees for meat and, as usual, I got wind of it and poked around the scene looking for items to either eat or use. The camel hide was a particularly hardy type of skin so I cut two large pieces for soles that were secured with long strips of thong I wrapped around my ankles and tied at the shin like a Roman gladiator.

I had also made my own shack in Ifo. At that time, I assumed my family and I, like most Sudanese refugees, would eventually end up in America, so I daubed the low-rise, mud-walled hut in white paint and promptly named it the White House. I was living there when I received a message from Aguil towards the end of 1995. There was a lot of movement among Sudanese refugees in the various camps and communities in Kenya, and Aguil had gotten wind that I was in Ifo. She explained that our family had been accepted for resettlement to a place called Australia and that I needed to return to Nairobi to prepare to leave. She even sent me the bus fare.

I didn't quite know what to make of the news at first. My aim until that point was to somehow still find a way back to Sudan. After a few days however, I started to feel intrigued. We'd be going to the white world after all, I thought to myself. Maybe that'd be a good thing. Maybe it would be different.

A few weeks later I reunited with my family as we faced a series of medical checks and blood tests to make sure we were all healthy and free of disease, most notably AIDS, which was rampant in East Africa.

During the countdown to our departure, I became more excited about the future – something I hadn't felt since I was a naked boy on the banks of the White Nile twelve years earlier. Ever since I became a boy soldier I had been tainted by fear and hatred. I felt like my future had been stolen from me and my dreams dashed. But Australia had suddenly appeared on the horizon, promising a fresh start. It was as if I was being handed a new life; I felt like I could start to dream again. This reversal of fortunes was so sudden and so profound that I had trouble comprehending it.

Just a few days before we were due to leave, though, the dream came crashing down when I took a look at the list of everyone in the family who'd be travelling to Australia: Aguil, myself, my brothers Deng and Garang, my youngest sister Akeer, my cousins Dew, Ruben, Ajak, and Aleer plus Aguil's young children, Dhieu, Dut and Agum.

'Why isn't Mum's name on the list?' I asked, thinking there must have been some kind of mistake.

'She'll be coming later,' Aguil told me. 'She's staying here for now.'

'WHAT?!' I exploded.

'She's coming later,' Aguil said coolly.

'No way!' I shouted. 'I will never leave here without Mum. I will not go.'

A family friend named Nyibol Riek had been helping us get organised for the trip and she did her best to explain the situation to me.

'Ayik, I want you to go to Australia,' she said gently. 'Just because your mum isn't going now doesn't mean that she won't go later. But if *you* don't go now this is the only chance you'll get – you might never get another one and your mum might never get to go there either.'

'But why isn't her name on the forms?' I countered. 'I don't know why she isn't going in the first place!'

'She wasn't put on the list because your sister was worried about taking care of you kids first,' Nyibol explained. 'Your mother is an adult – she can take care of herself here until you can go through the processes in Australia to have her join you. But Aguil needs to look after all the children first, especially the little ones. You need to go, Ayik. Australia will change your life.'

I hugged my mum and cried. She told me she would be OK.

On the day we were due to leave, Nyibol gave each of us a special parting gift – traditional African outfits made from brightly coloured material with bizarre pants that had the crotch down around the knees, topped off with a ridiculous-looking little hat.

'OK,' Nyibol said as she looked at us all dressed up in her idea of high fashion. 'Now you look ready to take on the world, African-style.'

9

'ME DANIEL!'

The only thing I knew for sure about Australia was that big fur-covered dinosaurs lived there. Australia's native kangaroos had heads that looked a bit like our African deer but they shared the huge hind legs and spindly arms with a Tyrannosaurus Rex. I'd seen a photo of one in a book at boarding school in Kapenguria but the picture didn't provide any scale. Because of its distinctive shape, I figured the kangaroo grew as tall as its scaly cousin, the T-Rex; maybe the height of an elephant. Definitely much bigger than a cow. Other than that, Australia was a mystery to me.

We flew from Nairobi to Zimbabwe and changed planes in Harare for the flight to Perth, which marked the first time any of us had been near an ocean, let alone sailing high above one inside an enormous metal tube.

Someone told me we were over the Indian Ocean but I couldn't see it from nearly ten thousand metres up.

About an hour after Africa fell away behind us some very nice flight attendants brought around trays of food. I sat up in my seat and excitedly pulled the cellophane wrapping off, only to be instantly repelled. Inside were two bits of doughy bread clamped around a thin, pinkish strip of something that stank of fish. I couldn't go near it for the smell. I began to worry that all food in Australia might smell that bad. What had we gotten ourselves into?

The Dinka way of cooking requires you to boil meat for hours and hours on end. The result is a stew that smells almost like thin air. Virtually all aroma from whatever you've cooked – be it meat, fish or whatever – is boiled out of existence. That was just fine by me because I hated the smell of fish.

'It's a ham sandwich,' the flight attendant told me, obviously reading the consternation on my face.

It may well have been a piece of pig, but to me it still smelled like fish. In fact all the food on that plane smelled like fish so I stuck to the little cups of sweet orange juice and the airline-sized biscuits instead, and prayed that Australians boiled things in giant pots, too.

I don't remember too much about our arrival in Perth other than we had to change planes again. One thing I'll never forget about my first very hours in Australia, however, is how self-conscious I felt thanks to my brightly coloured 'African' garb and my funny little hat. I felt like a clown. Everybody else at Perth Airport was in all manner of Western clothes. Women even wore jeans and short skirts – something I had never thought possible. Inside the terminal, all the Australians seemed to blend in with each other. The twelve of us, on the other hand, looked like a shiny rainbow that had fallen out of the sky and broken into pieces. I desperately wanted to get changed so I could disappear.

Later that night we flew across the Australian desert in darkness until the sound of the jet engines changed pitch and a voice in the roof said we were near our destination: a place called Brisbane.

All of us took turns pushing our faces against the windows to see what awaited us. From up in the night sky my first impression of Brisbane was of a brand new, sparkling universe: a starburst of what seemed like a billion twinkling lights in the blackness below.

Before I could fully comprehend this bizarre but beautiful cosmos, we were on the ground in Brisbane, Queensland, Australia. A different world, indeed. It was around 9 pm on 30 January 1996 but despite the late hour, the heat and stifling humidity came as a massive shock. When we left Nairobi it had been quite cool. By contrast, stepping out of the air-conditioned arrivals area in Brisbane was like walking into a cloud of hot vapour. I had to gasp to catch a good breath and dreaded to think how crazy hot it must get during the daytime.

We were met by some people from a church-based charity called Anglicare, who'd organised a minibus to collect us. As we had done in the descending plane, we all pressed our noses to the glass as the bus sped towards the shimmering city of Brisbane. I could not believe how many lights there were in my new home. Easily more than in all of Sudan and maybe even Kenya, too. Enormous buildings each had a thousand globes blazing away inside them.

We kept pinching and poking at each other to 'Look over there! Oh my God! Get a load of *that*!' There were bright lights along every single street. There were huge banks of lights in red, blue, green, yellow and pink on the tops and sides of buildings. Some made up pictures, or words I figured must have been English. There were even red, green and white lights winking in the sky as other plane-loads of lucky souls glided down into Brisbane.

Then there were the cars! There seemed to be millions of them: sleek, glossy, beautiful cars everywhere you looked. The minibus stopped at an intersection near the city and my brother pointed out a strange red light on a pole in the shape of a little person that was flashing on and off. 'Awww,' was all I could manage as we stared at it together. Suddenly the little man-light turned green and started making a weird chirping sound. Then, without warning, a big group of white people who had been just standing around by the side of the road walked across in front of us together! We could hardly comprehend it! Looking back now it's hard to believe the culture shock was so intense that something as pedestrian as a pedestrian crossing almost blew our minds.

Soon we arrived at a second-storey unit that Anglicare had arranged for us in Annerley, a suburb just south of the city. Back in the sticky sauna of the Brisbane night I again found it hard to breathe properly; the air felt wet in my lungs. As soon as we went inside I had to have a cool shower – the first of four I had that night.

When I re-emerged, everybody was crowded around the kitchen, where the doors to a refrigerator full of food were open. There were steaks, bread, drinks, vegetables and fruit – every kind of food you could think of. Someone was already cooking up a batch of sausages on top of a big, shiny white box. I had never seen so many sausages. Up until then I had encountered no more than six of the things throughout all my nineteen years.

Then someone handed me a plate laden with steaming, plump sausages and salad, or rabbit food as we called it. My brothers and I considered lettuce and tomatoes as nothing more than feed for African wildlife. Although my family were dedicated meat-eaters, things like steak and sausages were luxury items to us. A sausage had never passed my lips in Sudan and I had only tasted my first one a few years earlier while briefly living with Dr John Garang's well-to-do family in Kapenguria.

After all, we were just poor survivors of war. Even in Kenya while our refugee status was being processed, eight to ten of us at any one time crammed into Aguil's tiny two-bedroom unit. My last meal in Africa would have been typical of our average dinners: a couple of vegetables, some cabbage and maybe a bit of meat all boiled in a pot with a little bread to go with it. So a plate of juicy Australian sausages suddenly sitting in my lap was truly something to behold.

Thanks to the inedible plane food, I was starving by the time we got into Brisbane. The first sausage I downed quelled any fears I'd had about Australia's fishy-smelling food. It was delicious. I almost breathed the next one in, and the next, and the one after that. In the back of my mind I was thinking, This is too good! People can't eat like this every day! I figured this sausage-fest was obviously a customary banquet to welcome us to Australia. There would be no more sausages tomorrow – maybe even ever.

After I'd pushed maybe eight into my face, I felt sick and had to throw the sausages up in the toilet. Even though I'd eaten until I'd vomited, I ate some more straightaway because I didn't want the festival of meat to end. That night I slept on sheets that smelled like the white people's world – all perfumed and crisp.

My first morning in Australia dawned hot, humid and very, very strange. I stood on the balcony of the unit and took my first good look at this new world. God, it was weird. The sun had been up for a while but there was not a single soul out on the streets. Occasionally a car would murmur past but aside from that, the place looked and felt like a ghost town.

In Africa, the streets are filled from well before dawn until well after dark. People would wake up at 4 am and get busy. Some might be taking chickens to market, others could be carrying sacks of grain on their heads. Some would be bartering and trading, or there'd be groups of fifty people or more all heading somewhere together. Loads of them – women, children and men – all busy, all going somewhere, all of the time.

'Hey, I think we've been put somewhere where people

don't live,' I called out to my brothers as I took in the emptiness of suburban Annerley.

'No,' Aguil replied from the kitchen. 'This is white people's world. They've all got cars. Everything is organised.'

After a while I noticed some human activity in the street below, but Australia was still definitely freaky. Again I was struck by the way people dressed – particularly the women. I had only ever seen women either totally naked or wearing long dresses that covered them up. As strange as that may sound, in my mind if a woman was going to be clothed her only option was a dress. Everybody knew that! That was just common sense, right? Wrong. In Australia women could wear pants, tops, shorts, little skirts *and* dresses. In fact, they could wear whatever they wanted.

During the previous night's banquet I overheard one of the people from Anglicare say they'd be taking us to a place called Toowoomba in the morning. Apparently Toowoomba had a bigger house where all twelve of us could comfortably fit. Before long, we were back in the minibus and heading out of Brisbane along a flat highway under the blaring hot sun. If only I knew then what trouble I would find myself in on that stretch of road in the years that lay ahead . . .

That afternoon we arrived in Toowoomba, a pretty-looking city of eighty thousand people on a crest of the Great Dividing Range, a hundred and thirty kilometres west of Brisbane. The minibus drew to a stop outside a big house made out of chocolate-coloured bricks. Ludlow Court was in a quiet, leafy neighbourhood and the house was situated right across the road from a sprawling, grass-covered sanctuary called Toowoomba Bicentennial Waterbird Habitat. Before I could check it out the people from Anglicare ushered us inside our new home. Compared to the grass huts and single rooms we'd been crushed into most of our lives, the house had the feel of a palace. Its five bedrooms and several large living areas easily absorbed our entire bewildered family.

We were shown our beds, complete with mattresses, pillows and sweet, deodorised white people's sheets. We were all given clothes and properly introduced to a TV for the first time, and were told how to turn it on and change the channels. We were shown how the lights worked, how the taps and cook-tops worked, what a phone and a washing machine were and how to operate the microwave.

When they showed us the fridge I felt like I'd died and gone to heaven. Once again there were sausages inside – lots of sausages. They were arranged alongside steaks, bread, butter and all manner of Australian food and beverages. I quickly fell in love with the soft drinks. In Kenya you'd be lucky to get a drink of Sprite, Fanta or Coke at a rich person's home. In Australia, it looked like everyone could have it. That night, with the question of the national sausage supply settled in my mind, I didn't eat until I was sick.

Australia had put us all in a giddy, almost disbelieving state that was close to shock. The kindness of the people from the Anglican Church was hard to fathom. After just twenty-four hours in this country – following the grinding years in a war zone and enduring the poverty and fear of being refugees – we were suddenly being shown something far beyond care and respect. As far as I could see, we were being treated like royalty.

The next day, people arrived to take us to places that had names like Centrelink, Medicare and Supermarket. The place they called Woolworths was a cavernous room divided into about twenty hallways. The walls of each hallway were stacked high with different types of food and other luxuries wrapped in all kinds of bright packages! Unbelievable.

We discovered we were only the second family of refugees from the war in Sudan to settle in Toowoomba. It turned out we were as much of a novelty to the local white population as giant warehouses full of food were to us. People would turn to look at us as we blundered about in public in those early days. Most Australians were really nice to us, but some seemed a bit strange – a little hostile, even.

Eventually I would discover that racism can be a subtle thing in Australia – it's not always as overt and easy to spot as it is in Africa. Nowadays there are hundreds of South Sudanese families who call Toowoomba home but back in 1996 if you saw a black African in the street it was almost guaranteed to be my cousin, my brother, my sister, my nephew, my niece or me. As the Aussies would say, we stuck out like dog's balls.

Soon we crossed the road from the house to explore the beautiful public expanse that is the Toowoomba Bicentennial Waterbird Habitat. After just one afternoon in there I had a new name for it: Mormon Heaven. As soon as we walked through the gate I was vividly reminded of a drawing I'd seen in a refugee camp. It was in a booklet about the Mormon faith and it depicted what people could expect when they made it to heaven. It turned out the park across the road from my new house was a replica of the Mormons' idea of paradise. Happy white families sat on grassy hills that rolled gently down to a lake where mother ducks fussed over ducklings. Children in neat clothing bounded and played on pristine lawns. Parents laughed and smiled. Smiling old people tossed bread to the waterbirds and the sun shone like a god in an impossibly blue sky.

'I've seen this place before – in a book,' I told Ruben, who stood awestruck beside me on the bank of the lake. 'This is just what heaven will look like. We're lucky, I tell you. We're standing in paradise right now.'

There was, however, one thing that irked me about the idyllic scene: why on earth would anyone give perfectly good bread to birds? They don't need humans to feed them so why not let the ducks eat whatever and give the bread to a starving person? Aside from that, I was totally in love with Toowoomba. It was the most pristine, sparkling place I had ever been. At times I felt as if I'd been gently swept up by a giant hand, carried across the sky and placed into a new life: a glorious waking dream that literally looked like the promised land. Although I was anxious for my mum to join us I felt optimistic, excited and even happy.

If only the feeling could have lasted.

—

My father, Chut Deng Achouth, as a young man.

Aunty Dew, who protected me when I was a child soldier with the SPLA.

Here I am as a small boy (at right) with my brother Deng. *(All images on this page courtesy of Aguil Chut Deng)*

Me as a teenager (on the far left) with some of my fellow Red Army soldiers on the border of Uganda and Sudan. *(Author's collection)*

Kids with guns. Another group shot with the Red Army. I'm in the front row, second from the right. *(Author's collection)*

My school photo, taken when I was attending Centenary Heights State High School in Toowoomba. *(Author's collection)*

Posing for the camera. I was sure that this photo was going to launch my career as a model but I was totally wrong. At that point, I wasn't even thinking about acting. *(John Riedel)*

My family after arriving in Australia in 1996. Back row, from left: Aguil, Dew, Ruben, Garang, Akeer, me, Deng. Front row, from left: Agum, Dut, Dhieu, Aleer, Ajak. *(Author's collection)*

Hanging out with my brother Deng and Natalie, the niece of my former teacher John Riedel. *(John Riedel)*

Enjoying life by the pool in Toowoomba in the summer of 1996–7. *(John Riedel)*

Sharing a meal with John Riedel, who was so kind to my family and me during our early years in Australia. *(Ruben Aguin Manyok)*

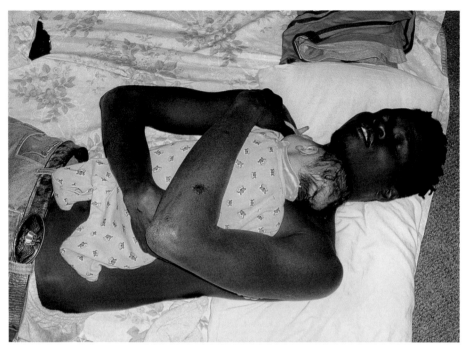

Becoming a father is the greatest thing that has happened to me. Here I am with my beloved son, who changed my life. *(Author's collection (above) and Ruben Aguin Manyok (below))*

My amazing sister Aguil. If it weren't for her, my family and I would still be in Sudan. She has done so much, both for my family and for the Sudanese community in Australia. I owe her everything. *(Author's collection)*

Me with my mother, Achol Aguin Majok. It was one of the happiest moments of my life when she was finally able to join the rest of my family in Brisbane. *(Temucin Mustafa)*

With the great Ray Martin at the filming of *Look Me in the Eye* in 2017. Since then, Ray has always managed to make time for me and I am honoured to call him a friend. *(Kelly Gardner)*

Pictured with me here is Sergeant Robert Duffner, the branch manager of the Fortitude Valley Police and Community Youth Club (PCYC) where I volunteer. Rob is a wonderful guy and I'm grateful for the opportunities that he has given me over the years, including allowing me to give back to the community. *(Temucin Mustafa)*

Pictured with me here is my great friend and mentor Temucin Mustafa, whose generosity and guidance has shaped my career as an actor. *(Lisa Melinda Polley)*

Here I am with Mum, my brother Garang, and my new friend Craig Henderson, a fantastic guy and the co-author of this book. *(Temucin Mustafa)*

Within a week I began Year 10 at Toowoomba's Centenary Heights State High School. I had been given a brand-new uniform and equipped with a new bag to carry my textbooks in. I was super excited and I took special care when dressing in my pale shirt and green shorts, all pressed and buttoned up nice and neat. A pair of shiny, black lace-up shoes completed my transformation into an Australian schoolboy. The only difference between me and the hundreds of other students who poured through the gate that morning was the fact I was a six-foot-two adult black man who couldn't speak their language.

Given my almost complete lack of education it was decided that starting me off in Year 11 or Year 12 would have doomed me to fail. I didn't care one bit; I was just happy to be at a school. I had hated the boarding school in Kenya because I felt like the other students looked down on me and resented my very presence. But in Toowoomba people seemed welcoming, even happy to see us. It filled me with hope. As I walked onto the grounds with my cousin Ruben and my brothers Garang and Deng I was in awe. Everything was so neat and so well organised. It was clear the entire operation was built for teaching and learning, unlike the schools under trees I was used to in Sudan. In that moment I felt a surge of excitement, like I had a real future.

'All my life I never dreamed I would have anything like this,' I mused as we were led across the playground to an orderly row of classrooms. 'You're at a *school* now. You can learn anything and be whatever you want.'

'Giddaymate. Owyagarn?' A squeaky voice interrupted my thoughts. I looked at my brothers in confusion and then down at the little white kid who smiled back at me expectantly. I hadn't understood a word he'd said. Soon he was joined by a couple of other scrappy youths of maybe fourteen or fifteen.

'Owyagarnmate?' said one.

'Wossyername, man?' the other little fellow piped up.

I was dumbfounded and must have looked it. The first boy seemed to cotton on and slowed his words waaay down for me. 'How. Are. You? What. Is. Your. Name?'

'Ahh! Me Daniel!' I said, touching my fingers to my chest and smiling back at him. 'Me Daniel! This brother! Me Sudanese!'

And with that first exchange I used up practically all of my available English. It was clear lots of kids wanted to make friends with us and they would try to hang around but for the longest time my communication was limited to little more than offering my name, rank and serial number. I was like one of those talking toy dolls with a nylon cord in the back that you pull to hear random recorded state-ments. *Z-z-zip*: 'Me child soldier!' *Z-z-zip*: 'Me Sudanese!' *Z-z-zip*: 'Me Daniel!'

It grew more and more frustrating as the weeks wore on. If someone asked me what part of Sudan I was from I couldn't answer them.

'What was the war about?'

'Who started the war, mate?'

'Did you kill anyone?'

I badly wanted to talk to the Australian kids and hear about their lives, too, but all I could do was reach behind my back and pull the cord. *Z-z-zip*: 'Me child soldier!'

My sisters went to a different school and my little niece and nephews were enrolled in a local primary school. They seemed to find it much easier to communicate and assimilate than I did. Since they were much younger than me, all they really needed to do was run around with other little kids in the neighbourhood and, just like that, they suddenly had friends. As the oldest of the boys, I really struggled to fit in. My brothers and Ruben were in Years 8 and 9 but they appeared to be doing much better than me, too. After all, I was nineteen – three years older than my classmates and a whole world apart in where my head was at.

Sometimes after school I'd cross the road to sit alone in Mormon Heaven and weep with frustration. The next moment my little nephews would appear with a soccer ball and a basketball, squealing with some white Aussie kids in tow, and I'd be reminded that although I was having a hard time fitting in and understanding lessons being taught to me in a foreign language, I was still living in paradise and there were no Didinga militiamen hiding in the bushes with AK-47s aimed at my head.

Gradually I started to learn more English and – just as importantly – how Australians used the language. In Africa, English is spoken much more deliberately. Each word is delivered crisply. In Toowoomba, however, sentences like 'Good day. What are you doing? Do you want some help?' were hurried into a blur of syllables, then compressed and flattened until they came out as 'G'day. Watcha doowen? Ya wansome elp?' It would be quite a while before I could decipher more complex propositions like, 'Garnuptha baskaball court sarvo, man. Yezwanna come?' Truly learning the local lingo would take me many years. I'm pretty bloody good at it nowadays but I've still got a long way to go.

English wasn't the only thing I found hard to get my head around. Coming from a strong farming background I was very good with my hands so I did quite well in woodwork, metalwork and agriculture studies. But because I truly wanted to excel in my new life I had decided to dedicate myself to science and mathematics, too. Australia was the land of opportunity, where I could become anything I wanted – if I worked hard enough. Since Dad had been some kind of doctor I thought I might start a family tradition by becoming a medico: Dr Ayik.

The sciences proved virtually impossible for me, though. I had come off a frightfully low academic base in Africa, as my misguided ideas about kangaroos showed. Launching straight into the complexity of even basic physics, biology and chemistry without having a handle on English was always destined to end in failure and frustration.

I was so hopeless that one day I accidentally set fire to the science room. I had mixed the wrong chemicals and a Bunsen burner was involved. Suddenly, with a *whoomph!* sound, flames leaped across the desk. Everyone panicked and the teacher had to evacuate us all in case the whole lab exploded.

Thankfully, I excelled in one area: sport. I loved soccer, basketball and cross-country running, and I eventually represented the school in regional competitions. One Western sport I thought ridiculous, though, was walking, and I laughed out loud at the idea. After all, I had walked across much of East Africa just to stay alive. You don't do it for fun, I thought.

But even my successful school sporting career had gotten off to a typically rocky, refugee-like start. I had a pair of prized new soccer boots and on the morning of our first sports day I proudly laced them on with the rest of my school uniform. I walked two kilometres to school in the things and then from class to class, clacking awkwardly along the hallways. I attracted quite a few looks, but nobody had told me you were supposed to take them to school in your bag and put them on when it was time for sport. By the time I got to play soccer that day I was totally crap because my feet were absolutely killing me.

On top of the cultural quirks and the language barrier, girls provided another major source of distraction and frustration for me. All day long I was surrounded by beautiful Australians: blonde girls, brunette girls, red-headed girls. Every corner I'd walk around: *boom*. There'd be another girl. Naturally I couldn't stop thinking about them but I had no idea how to converse with them, let alone show any interest beyond just staring at them, which I quickly learned wasn't the done thing.

The customs surrounding courtship in Africa were nothing like the Australian way. In Dinka culture, girls are selected for marriage. It would be a matter of your father talking it over with her father: 'I think I want my son to marry your daughter in the future.' There's no way a Dinka man could just wander up to a girl and say, 'Hey, how are you doing? Would you like to go out sometime?' Her family would beat the shit out of you.

If you liked a girl back in the village when you were thirteen or fourteen, the best you could do was secretly follow her about from a discreet distance and sometimes throw her a sneaky little wave. If her father or uncles caught you doing that you'd still get belted from one end of the village to the other, so the idea of just sitting down on the couch and eating popcorn with a girl after school was inconceivable.

Another massive difference was the complete absence of kissing in Dinka-style romance. I never once saw my mum and dad share a kiss – ever. In fact I'd never seen any Sudanese people kissing, period. People's lips simply did not meet in our world, so the first time I saw a boy and girl kiss at Centenary Heights High I had no idea what they were doing. I only knew it was one of the most shocking, bizarre, revolting rituals I had ever witnessed.

At our school the young couples would make out in the relative privacy of the basketball courts, where Ruben, my brothers and I could usually be found shooting hoops and trying to look like our new hero, Michael Jordan. As soon as the smooching started we'd be struck aghast. 'Argh!

Look at that!' we'd say, nudging each other as little lovers locked lips. 'That's just disgusting, man! They eat food with their mouths and then they go and do that? Oh my God! *Yuck*!'

No one in our family could believe the kissing plague that swept Australia. Every time we'd watch a film at home we'd all gee each other up and say, 'Yeah there's going to be kissing in this movie.' Sure enough there'd be some scene between a man and a woman, the music would go all sweet and sappy, and the kissing would start. '*Yuuuck!*' we'd holler as one. What was it about white people and all this kissing? Well, as the Australians say, 'Don't knock it until you've tried it.' Eventually I started kissing girls, too, and I came to realise that where we came from, everyone was missing out on something very, very special.

My first year in Toowoomba was a long, slow, confusing indoctrination and adjustment to the orderly, comfortable and safe world I had miraculously found myself living in. Now and then, if I heard a plane flying low, a car back-firing or some fireworks going off I'd feel a familiar stab of adrenaline and instinctively look for somewhere to take cover. But even that wartime muscle memory started to fade a little. I felt like I was settling in and I was gaining a little confidence, too. I was even starting to learn to speak a little like an Aussie, eh?

By the end of Year 10 I'd passed metalwork and woodwork and also logged a 'sound achievement' in agricultural science. Every other subject, however, was a complete disaster. I failed English, mathematics, science and geography – dismally. The most frustrating aspect of this failure was the fact I'd studied diligently and worked hard in class all year. I concentrated at school. I did all my homework and I never missed a single day. Despite the bad results, I was awarded my Year 10 Leaving Certificate but I wasn't going anywhere; I vowed to return in 1997 to tackle Year 11 with even more determination to succeed than ever before.

I just hoped my recurring nightmares would stop.

10

CHASED BY A WAR

I always heard the blowflies before I saw them. The hum would grow louder as they swarmed overheard and dipped ever closer to my rotting corpse. I was somewhere in the African bush and I'd been shot. I could smell my body's decay, which meant I must be dead. But maybe, if I tried as hard as I could to open my eyes, I might just come back from the afterworld before the blowflies laid their eggs and the maggots consumed me. 'Open your eyes, Ayik. Open your eyes, man, and you might live.' It took all of my will to haul my heavy eyelids back up in my skull, but when I did, I was relieved to find I was safe and sound in my bed in Toowoomba. I could still hear the blowflies, though, until I realised it was the drone of traffic on the main road that ran behind our house.

The nightmares began after I'd been in Toowoomba for about a year. Each time it was the same and I would

135

always rationalise it later as my unconscious mind processing things I'd seen in the war: nothing to worry about too much. OK, I *had* been shot at many times so that was real, but my skin was never once pierced by a bullet. I didn't die and I didn't rot in the ground to become maggot food. Bad dreams aren't real so I just tried to shake them off and get through my day. I sure as hell never told anyone about them. That just wasn't the African way; we kept all our shit to ourselves and never spoke of what we'd been through. Not once.

Although I was having to do battle with these nocturnal demons I was once again excited about the school year. As a senior, I was still fixated on a future as a medical professional so I elected to study chemistry, physics and engineering technology. You'd think I would have learned, but I still had the attitude that if I simply applied myself as best as I could in the Lucky Country, I would be rewarded with a good career and a happy life.

Again, I worked hard at school and just as hard at home. I gave it one hundred per cent and then some. We even had a tutor, a stunningly beautiful blonde girl in her twenties named Samantha. She was like a Barbie doll who'd been dropped into our lives straight from heaven. In Africa, everybody's eyes are dark but Samantha had piercing, extraordinarily bright blue eyes. She reminded me of a cat. We would each go to her office for one-on-one tutoring sessions but when it was my turn I'd get all flustered.

I had an intense crush on Samantha but even with that distraction I took the work seriously and applied myself doubly hard to improve my grades. While my younger family members progressed well, I found I was still infuriatingly stuck in academic first gear. In neutral, actually.

Up until then, home life in Ludlow Court had been reasonably calm and organised, despite us all making the odd rookie Westerner mistake. In my case, it was almost blowing up the microwave by accidentally nuking a spoon. For the first year in Australia I dedicated a lot of my free time to catch-up eating, trying all the food I'd missed out on in my African life.

I grew used to lots of new and different Western food and found much of it pretty palatable. However, there were some things Aussies put in their mouths that we found utterly disgusting. The first time I saw an Australian eating mushrooms, for instance, I nearly gagged. In Dinka, the mushroom is universally referred to as 'hyena's dick' – a filthy protuberance that must never pass the lips.

Nowadays I love nothing more than hyena's dick gravy with a meal but back in the '90s we mostly ate meat with meat and more meat. If we weren't cooking meat we were cutting it up, or going out to buy some more. The four of us older ones handled the cooking while the eight little ones did the housework, vacuuming and tidying up. Even though I was living in a household of twelve, nothing really bugged me except when my family spoke to each other in the Dinka language in public.

'Hey! Stop that!' I would chastise them. 'We need to speak English because we're in Australia now, not Sudan!'

But there was another reason I wanted them to use the local lingo, beyond just a longing to assimilate as quickly as possible. I worried that if we spoke Dinka in public, the white people would think we were secretly talking about them – and they wouldn't like it.

This paranoia had its roots in the days I'd spent running for my life all over Africa. I just knew that when people in other countries spoke in their native dialects they were talking shit about me. They'd rattle off a few indecipherable sentences then stare at me and sometimes even spit on the ground as a filthy exclamation mark.

'Just talk like you're Australians, man!' I'd tell my brothers and Ruben as they chattered away in Dinka while we walked to school.

But those guys were already experimenting with being 'niggaz'. Hip-hop had exploded in the 1990s and, understandably, the boys were taking some of their cultural cues from MTV and American rap artists. I'd sometimes hear them talk about homies, dawgs, bling-bling and cribs. All that meant nothing to me; I was in Toowoomba, not Compton, and I wanted to speak like a real Aussie, not Tupac bloody Shakur. Deep down I desperately wanted to *be* a real Aussie.

One of the early things I learned, with some help from some Australian classmates, was how to swear properly. I had noticed that swearing was an important feature of Australian interpersonal communication. It could be used to emphasise a point or to enhance humour. Usually when I tried it out on my brothers it was to emphasise a point:

'Just talk in English, ya fucken dickheads!' I implored them, albeit with a strong Sudanese accent.

Funnily enough, the one Australianism I refused to try to adopt was the one the nation was most famous for: the noun 'mate'. I would hear people say it fifty times a day: G'day, mate. How ya goin', mate? Good onya, mate. Yeah, mate. Nah, mate. Mate, mate, mate, mate, mate. As naturally as it comes to born-and-bred Aussies, I noticed foreigners had to force 'mate' out of their mouths sideways. It was totally unconvincing. As soon as I heard myself saying 'mate' I knew it sounded all wrong so I swore off it forever. Besides, when I looked up the definition of mate in the dictionary it said, 'The sexual partner of a bird or animal.'

Of course, in time I would realise that not all Australians used the word mate or swore, and barely any would think people conversing in a foreign language were secretly talking about them. For a while I thought Australia was full of mostly white people and just a tiny smattering of us blacks. It took a while for it to dawn on me that Australia is one of the world's great multicultures: a nation first populated by ancient Indigenous peoples, which is now home to immigrants of all different colours from all across the globe. Even awkward, towering young men from the land of blacks.

—

Vzzzzzzzzzz . . .

The blowflies were swarming thicker now. Yet again I'd been shot; the dried blood caked on my ruptured skin was crawling with flies and maggots. I looked up from my tomb in the African sand and saw vultures corkscrewing down out of the sky to join the feast – a true sign I was really dead this time.

'Open your eyes and you might live,' my voice called to me from somewhere far away. 'Open your eyes, man. Do it now!' A few minutes later I was up, brushing my teeth and getting ready for school.

Something was definitely wrong with me. The nightmares were one thing but they only happened when I was asleep so I could cope with them, just. On top of experiencing my own death, my dreams filled up with the blood, guts and mangled flesh I had seen during the war. About halfway through Year 11, however, the horrible visions spilled over into my waking hours. Strangely, the hallucinations centred on household cooking duties.

One day after school, Aguil asked me to cut up some meat for the stewing pot. No big deal; I'd done it a hundred times before. But that afternoon as I sliced into the slippery purple slabs of gravy beef, I had a vivid, horrifying vision of the knife blade cutting into the bodies of my little family members who were giggling and watching TV in the next room. I tried to blink the awful image out of my mind. Maybe I'm just tired or something, I tried to reason, and returned to the cutting board. But the more I sliced and diced, the more I felt like I was hacking into my little loved ones. I grew faint and dizzy and had to walk across the road to Mormon Heaven to gather myself. I knew the visions weren't real and that the kids were unharmed and perched safe and sound in front of the telly, but the experience really rattled me.

Being a Dinka man, I didn't say a word about it to anyone or explain my behaviour to my family. Doing so would have been a sign of weakness and completely un-African. I thought that if I told them I was having nightmares about being dead they would laugh at me. Although my younger brother Deng had also served as a child soldier, we never once spoke about what we went through in Sudan – even though we shared the same room. I knew everyone in my family had endured their own suffering during the war, too, but I figured they must be having their own nightmares and dealing with it in the African way, which is to just shut up and keep it to yourself. Still, after that ghoulish aberration in the kitchen I dreaded being asked to cut up the meat.

I had witnessed some atrocious things during the war: people being maimed and killed in front of me, not to mention the macabre human aftermath that was almost everywhere you looked in Sudan. It was not uncommon to travel along a road and see corpses and even stray body parts in various states of decomposition. Some cadavers would be freshly dead with crimson innards exposed. Others would be like bony husks topped with sunken heads and bulging, lifeless eyes. It was nothing to see vultures perched atop the dead, methodically pecking and tearing at the softer body parts. Sometimes you'd catch flashes of white in the bush – skulls and skeletons that had been bleached by the sub-Saharan sun. Those were the memories that suddenly decided to crash back into my life just in time for dinner in Toowoomba.

'Ayik, you need to cut up the meat,' Aguil called out the next time we were cooking a stew.

'No. Get one of the others to do it,' I replied. 'I'll fry the onions and put the lentils in but I'm not cutting up any meat.'

Aguil had no idea of the reasons behind my sudden refusal to help – she just thought I was being an arsehole. 'No, no, no!' she said, waving her finger at me. '*You* have to do it!'

I begrudgingly picked up the knife and started chopping into the big lumps of lamb and the flashbacks started right on cue. Staring down at the kitchen bench I could see bits of mangled human and the blood-drenched aftermath of an Arab bombing run. Again, each stroke of the blade was like inflicting mortal wounds on the sweet, innocent kids in the next room. I started to tremble. I wanted to cry and it felt like I was being chased around the kitchen by the war.

'FUCK!' I screamed and stabbed the knife upright into the chopping board before stomping out of the house and into the twilight. I was unravelling.

One morning, the news reported that Princess Diana had been killed in a car crash along with her boyfriend, Dodi Fayed. As I watched the TV coverage about these people I didn't even know, I found myself completely consumed by grief. I wept like a child; sheets of tears poured down my face as my bemused brothers and sisters tried to console me.

'What's the matter with you? Why are you so upset?' they wanted to know.

I had no answer, only more tears. I'd heard of Princess Di before and I knew she had been working to clear landmines from parts of Africa so maybe my grief over her death was a proxy for all the souls I had seen ripped apart before my own eyes? I didn't really know.

Sometimes I cried for other people I didn't know – the boy who'd stared into my soul as he drowned in the river near Raad and all the frail boys who'd died of disease in Dimma. And I wept for their families, too – all of them strangers to me.

My fragile temperament continued to weaken until one day when Aguil told me to cut up some meat and I exploded like an anti-tank grenade. I smashed up the kitchen and screamed at the top of my lungs. Still oblivious to the waking hell of my flashbacks, Aguil seemed shocked, appalled and angry about my sudden volcanic eruption. She was probably frightened, too. She had no idea about what was going on with me and she still doesn't as I write these words. My kitchen rampage was enough for Aguil to call the police – my first, but not my last, encounter with the boys in blue. Up until then, the only police I knew were the *Blue Heelers* on the television.

—

Virtually every teacher at Centenary Heights High was very nice to me, but one stood out above all others. His name was John Riedel. John was a relief teacher and the first time I saw him in the playground he gave me a warm smile and asked how I was doing. The next time I spoke to John was at the school basketball courts one weekend in mid-1997.

On most Sunday afternoons, like a lot of the local kids, my brothers, cousin and I would head to the courts to shoot hoops and just hang out. One day, the other kids left early but we stayed behind to practise. The next thing I knew the nice teacher, John Riedel, had arrived, accompanied by his young nephew. We all played basketball until it grew dark and cold. John asked me if we needed a lift home.

'Yes, please,' I said, nodding.

When he dropped us off in Ludlow Court, John handed me a piece of paper with his name and phone number scribbled on it. 'If you ever need anything,' he said as I climbed out of the car, 'just give me a call, OK?'

A month or so later I did just that. I explained to John that Aguil had thrown me out of the house after I busted up the kitchen and refused to cut the meat for dinner, the police had arrived and could he please come over. True to his word, he didn't hesitate. He made it there in under ten minutes. John helped calm the situation and explained to the police that ours was a family of refugees from the war in Sudan and there was no danger to anyone; it was just a family disagreement over who was cooking the dinner.

I was very grateful for John being there to help smooth things out. The situation needed someone with a cool head to explain it. Sadly, his intervention was only a temporary fix. Staying silent and stoic about my nightmares and gruesome dinnertime visions didn't make them go away.

The next time I blew up and Aguil kicked me out I called on John again and I ended up going to live with him and his lovely mum Mavis in another part of Toowoomba.

Just like the people from Anglicare who welcomed us to Australia, John and Mavis were among the most patient and caring humans I had ever met. They took me in, gave me a room of my own and fed me. They even let me make expensive international calls to Nairobi so I could speak to Mum any time I wanted, which was almost every day. In less than a year I had racked up a $700-plus phone bill but they didn't care – they were just happy I could talk to my mother.

I took to calling Mavis 'Mum' because she fulfilled that caring, nurturing role in my life at that time. I was shattered when, in the winter of 1997, Mavis passed away at the age of eighty following complications from an operation. I went to see her in hospital before she died and grew very upset because she was unconscious. I had lost many people in Africa but Mavis was the first person I knew in Australia who had died. It hurt just as much.

I found I was spending more and more time with white people. I was living with a white family, going to a white school and – after I got my first car – I even kissed a white girl. She asked me to pick her up one day so we could 'go for a drive' together. I obeyed and after she directed me to a secluded lookout she leaned in and kissed me! I tried to kiss her back like the leading men I had seen in the movies but it wasn't at all good. The whole thing was far too slimy for my liking and she had the smell of white people's food in her mouth.

145

The four of us African boys came in for a lot of attention from girls at school. I even had two girls fight over me, and not just any argument – it was a full-on fight with punching and kicking. I was bewildered by the attention. Culturally, none of us knew how to react.

Another girl had lost her mind over Ruben and followed him everywhere for a month. She eventually slipped a love note into his locker, which, sadly for her, did the opposite of winning his heart. Ruben was a Dinka boy and in his world, having an unauthorised relationship with a girl could land him in trouble. He reacted in the African way: he got up in the girl's face and bellowed at her to leave him alone. A female teacher saw his performance and stepped in.

'Excuse me, what's going on?' she asked. The girl and her giggling friends said Ruben had just blown up without reason.

'Is that right, Ruben?' the teacher asked.

Again, Ruben reacted in the Dinka way – he towered above the little white teacher and screamed while making wild, angry gestures. In his mind he had been seriously harassed by the girl and now again by the teacher. But the woman was so shaken that the police were called. Who knows – it could have been a wonderful teenage romance, but it was derailed before it could even begin by a simple clash of cultures.

Other episodes of confusion were more comical. In order to study – and also to avoid the black-guy version of Beatlemania we were living through – between classes we often retreated to the quiet of the school library. The librarian was a nice teacher named Mr Kirkwood but some of the students had worked out us Sudanese guys had trouble pronouncing his name. When we said it, it sounded less like Mr Kirkwood and more like Mr Cockhead.

'Ruben, go and ask Mr Cockhead if he can locate this book, will you?' Ruben's cheeky classmates prompted him one day.

Thinking nothing untoward, Ruben walked up to the librarian and asked for help. 'Hello Mr Cockhead. Can you please help me find this book?' The library erupted with the roar of teenage laughter.

Mr Kirkwood was a good guy and he let it slide, but my favourite teacher by far was still the relief teacher John Riedel. It turned out that, like me, John had lost his father at a relatively young age so he understood what it was like for a young man to grow up without an older male to lean on and look up to. Over the years I would lean on John a lot, but I wasn't the only one who benefited from knowing the big-hearted educator.

John took an interest in the wellbeing of my entire family and on many weekend nights after basketball Garang, Deng, Ruben and I would go back to John's place for much-anticipated and highly celebrated pizza nights. He helped me a lot with my English and he was the first person in Australia I was really able to tell about my childhood in Sudan and what I'd been through during the war. He was also the first person to recommend I see a psychologist.

'It might be a good idea to sit down and talk with someone who knows how to help with this stuff, mate,' he told me one night.

'Nah, John. I'm OK. It's not that bad. I'll be all right. Really.' A typically African shutdown.

Meanwhile at school, there were signs that I wasn't OK. In woodwork and metalwork I had set myself the assignment of making a gun. I used the bandsaw to fashion a pistol shape out of wood then made a barrel out of metal pipe. Using a firing mechanism I'd constructed with a motorbike spoke and an elastic piece of bike inner-tube I was soon re-armed and ready to go. I crossed the road into Mormon Heaven and tested the weapon, using crushed up match heads as homemade gunpowder. The thing worked but only just. After I fired a few nail 'bullets' into the bushes with a weak fizzle, I soon gave up.

Looking back, I wished I had taken John's advice about getting help. Maybe it would have saved me from all the heartache and trouble that was lying in wait for me and those I love.

I stayed with John for the rest of Year 11 and I worked really hard at school. No matter how much effort I put in, though, I couldn't lift my grades one bit. At least my conversational English was improving, thanks to the kids at school, and I had started to make a few good friends.

I spent a lot of time with a classmate named Reagan. He was a great guy and he had a car, too. He showed me how to jump the school fence at lunchtime so we could go to a local charity to get free sausage sandwiches. Reagan had a lot of great tricks like that up his sleeve and we had some fun times together.

I'd get invited to parties on the weekends, too, but I always declined. To me, those years were about school and studying hard so I could make a good life for myself. I hadn't given up on the idea that I might still get to be Dr Ayik. Even if I didn't accept people's party invitations, it was nice that they asked me.

I didn't necessarily get along with everyone, though. Sometimes it took me weeks to realise the words some Aussies were calling me were meant to hurt me. Once I did, not having the confidence or the linguistic sophistication I do now, I at least once resorted to an African-style slap to show them how I felt about it.

Since my earliest time in the tribe I had always confronted bullies head-on so to me it was normal to lash out at a perceived threat or insult. Slowly, though, I learned a better way of dealing with bullies: with humour, the Aussie way. But at school I felt I had no option other than to physically stop a bully in his tracks. Not everyone was racist, of course, but there were some kids I'd hear sniggering and I'd catch snippets and asides peppered with what I imagined must be slurs. The thing is, I didn't always know what these words really meant. It was a matter of what you didn't hear didn't hurt you, which was probably a good thing. Besides, there'd be plenty of time for hurt later on.

11

NO MODEL CITIZEN

My results in Year 11 were worse than they'd been in Year 10. Not even Samantha, the Barbie doll from heaven, could help me lift my grades. My relationship with Aguil was still strained and at the beginning of Year 12 I moved in with another family in Toowoomba. I'd become friends with a classmate, Sonia, who knew I was having family troubles so she asked her parents if I could move into their house. The next thing I knew I was an honorary family member, living with Sonia, her parents, Mark and Marie, and her younger brother, Mark John.

They were a family of what you'd call 'true blue Aussies'. Mark was a knockabout motor mechanic and on the weekends he loved a drink. A Jim Beam man, he had arranged his treasured bottles of bourbon in a cabinet in the lounge room like a kind of art installation-cum-shrine. Unlike John Riedel, whose house was one of quiet routine, this family was typical of middle-class Australians who worked hard during the week and played hard once Friday night rolled around. They were wonderful, salt-of-the-earth people who were warm, hospitable and kind beyond words to open their hearts and their home to me.

Mark loved motor sports and had a couple of old-school muscle cars he was always tinkering away on, including one V8 that roared like a tank whenever he fired it up. I remained laser-focused on my studies, knowing Year 12 was my final chance to do well in school. On the weekends, though, I received a different kind of education. I'd often join Mark and Mark John in front of the TV to watch the V8 Supercars, Formula One, the 500cc bikes – any sport that involved men and machines hurtling around a race-track. Before long, I was something of a petrolhead myself. I watched my first ever Bathurst 1000 with them and since then I've rarely missed the great race.

Mark liked a drink or two while he was watching the cars. I can't remember whether it was a special occasion or not but one day I decided to give this Aussie-style drinking thing a go. I went out and bought my own bottle of Jim Beam, took it back to the house and started throwing it down the hatch. For some reason, I thought when Africans drank spirits it was customary to have it neat. White people were always tipping Coke and other sweet mixers into their spirits but I was determined to drink mine straight up.

The first blast of foul-tasting elixir gushed down my throat like liquid fire and it almost came straight back up. Somehow I persisted and that afternoon I managed to pour the bottle's entire contents into my boiling gut. Up until that day I had only had a few slugs of home-brewed African beer, so downing a full bottle of a 40 per cent alcohol spirit in the hot Queensland sun was quite a step up.

The results of this insane baptism of fire-water were catastrophic. Aside from becoming paralytic, I spewed so much and so convulsively that I expected my stomach and intestines to fly out of my mouth with every burst of projectile vomit. Each individual cell in my body felt marinated in poison and I was bedridden for days afterwards, too sick to even go to school.

'Mate, that's why you mix it with Coke,' Mark John pointed out later.

—

In 1998 I finally left high school with marks so low I didn't even get my Senior Certificate, let alone have the faintest chance of becoming a respected medical doctor. Fortunately, the fertile regions that ringed Toowoomba – the Lockyer Valley to the east and the Darling Downs to the west – gave me an alternative that suited my Dinka farmer roots.

For the previous two years I had worked on farms during the school holidays. There was no shortage of employment for a strong, willing fruit-and-vegetable picker like me on the great food-producing plains of southern Queensland. I was earning $100 a day for chipping cotton or picking broccoli, tomatoes, onions and apples. In one block of mid-year holidays alone I could earn $1400 cash, most of which I sent back to Africa to help support my mum, who was still languishing in Nairobi. I missed her terribly and was desperate for her to join us in Australia but the process was slow. In the meantime, sending money was all I could do for her.

With my fleeting high school years now behind me, I travelled to the tiny town of Millmerran, which is smudged into the Darling Downs, about two hundred kilometres west of Brisbane. I'd worked there before on a family-run chicken farm and had stayed in touch with them. I'd also struck up something of a budding relationship with Kristy, the daughter of one of the farmers. When I returned in 1999 they were only too happy to put me on as a general farmhand.

Compared with the city of Toowoomba, Millmerran was little more than a collection of iron-roofed buildings, one old pub, three cops and maybe one thousand residents. I was the first black African most of the townspeople had ever seen in real life; I was certainly the first one to wander onto their little corner of the map.

My main job at Millmerran was to look after the chickens. I mixed the feed, made sure the birds were fed and watered and locked away safely at night. Occasionally I had to dispose of dead ones, too. When I discovered there was a gun on the property, I told the family I had experience with weapons and offered to go spotlighting at night to shoot any foxes that threatened to devour the clucking ladies.

'Sure, go for it!' was the reply.

The gun was a bolt-action .22 rifle – a standard tool found on most farms in Australia. It definitely had fewer moving parts than the AK-47s I was used to. One day I was outside the house with Kristy, showing her how good I was at handling weapons when *CRACK* – I bumped the trigger and the bloody thing went off in my hands. Kristy was standing right in front of me and nearly had a heart attack. Fortunately I'd had the good sense to hold the gun with the barrel pointing skywards so the bullet flew harmlessly to the heavens, way above Kristy's pretty head. My Red Army safety training had come to the fore, but she never let me hear the end of it.

Kristy was the first proper girlfriend I ever had. I'd messed about a little with some girls in high school but I never had anyone serious before. Kristy and I became very close as I started to let her into my heart and told her a little about my life in Sudan. After the mishap with the rifle I explained to her that I used to be a soldier and a gun-runner who'd once been armed and dangerous in the middle of a brutal civil war. I told her how I used to kill things for no reason, just shoot at birds in the bush with a pistol, mow bigger birds down with an AK or shoot monkeys just because I could. It didn't matter what I told her, though, Kristy said she loved me and we were together, so I was safe. I fell very deeply in love with her, too.

Despite our mutual affection, though, I sometimes felt like I was a bit of a novelty in Kristy's life. Any time we'd go to a party with her friends I'd be the only black person there. I'd overhear her girlfriends saying things like 'Oh, your boyfriend is cute!' And 'Where did you find him?' Or 'I've never seen a guy so black!' They were being nice, but I couldn't help but feel a little like I was a specimen from Mars out there on the Darling Downs.

I also had to get used to the idea of kissing, which I still considered bizarre and disgusting – especially if Kristy had been drinking alcohol. Following the great bourbon poisoning in Toowoomba I had vowed to never drink again but Kristy didn't mind a drop when she was out with her mates. She was also a social smoker, which made kissing her extra challenging. Not that Kristy wasn't a lovely girl, but the thought of locking lips and tongues with all that saliva, *and* the taste and smell of alcohol *and* cigarettes was almost too much for me to bear.

'Kristy,' I would tell her, 'if you're going to drink and try to kiss me, can you please brush your teeth?'

Other times I would tell her, 'No kissing at all today!'

She persisted, and gradually I grew used to kissing. Now I can quite happily kiss a woman if she's downed ten wines and smoked a box of cigars.

Although I was still sending money back to Mum in Nairobi, I eventually saved up enough to buy myself a better car. I'd started driving 'paddock bashers' on the chook farm in Millmerran and ended up getting my full licence right there in the town.

This set of wheels was a second-hand 1987 Ford Falcon XF sedan. It was a big, white brick of a thing with a powerful six-cylinder engine. Mark and Mark John's love of muscle cars had rubbed off on me and I made sure my Ford had fat tyres wrapped around a set of shiny mag wheels. I loved that car and it marked the beginning of my long, stupid love affair with driving as if I were Michael Schumacher and public roads were a Grand Prix circuit.

Now and then, Kristy and I would pile into the Ford and head down to the bright lights in the big city of Brisbane. One time, as we were passing through Toowoomba, I was pulled over and breathalysed by the police – a process that was completely alien to me. I rolled my window down as the cop approached.

'Sir, you've been stopped for a random breath test. Have you had anything to drink today?' the officer asked.

'Yes. Yes I have,' I replied truthfully.

'How much have you had to drink?'

'Oh, I don't know. A lot, I would say.'

'What have you had to drink exactly?'

'Well, I had a lot of milk at breakfast. Then I had some more milk after that and I have also had water. Mostly milk, though.'

I don't know if the cop thought I was being a smartarse or not but I passed his breathalyser and he let us go on our way. The next time I encountered an RBT it would not be such a laughing matter.

After about a year of working on the farm, Kristy and I decided to move to the big smoke permanently. After all, we were young and Millmerran was, well, kind of old. With a degree in medicine off the table I had started to think that maybe I could work as a model or a movie extra. Kristy was forever telling me how handsome I was and how exotic

I looked. Other people said they could see me working on TV or in ads, too. I also liked the idea of using the thing that made me different from everyone else – my skin – as a way of forging a future for myself. Kristy was right behind me.

'There's gotta be plenty of work in the city for you,' she insisted. 'You could model, easily!'

Even Kristy's mum was confident we'd be better off in Brisbane. 'Someone like you can work in a store,' she assured me. 'You can do anything, mate! You're strong, you're young, you're tall and good-looking. I reckon the city would be good for you.'

On one trip Kristy had taken it upon herself to organise an audition for me to kickstart my modelling career.

'Hey, you can dance, can't you, Dan?' she asked me.

'I'm from Africa, Kristy,' I said. 'We are born dancing.'

'Cool,' Kristy said, 'because I saw an ad in the paper for fit young guys to audition as dancers for this company. It looks really promising and I just know that once they see you they'll want to hire you.'

It sounded great to me. I had visions of working as a dancer in video clips or in movies and, who knows, maybe that would lead to work as an extra in the movies. The audition was scheduled for 7 pm at an address in Fortitude Valley, Brisbane's famous hub for bars, nightclubs and 'adult entertainment'. I felt excited and a little nervous, but confident I could make a good impression at the audition. Who knows? I thought. This could even end up being my big break.

We stepped inside what turned out to be some kind

of nightclub and walked up to the young woman at the reception desk. Kristy explained that we were there for my audition as a dancer while I looked around the club and saw a sea of writhing women clapping their hands and squealing in delight as they ogled a tanned, muscled white guy in a G-string gyrating and shaking his arse all over the place. I glared incredulously at Kristy who had a sheepish look on her face. We were back outside on the footpath in under a minute.

'Kristy! What were you thinking?' I said. 'That's not what I came here for! I thought this was about TV or the movies, not showing my body to women! Even though we walk naked in my tribe, we don't do that for money!'

Poor Kristy. She was a country girl who, like me, was way out of her depth in the fast-paced world of Fortitude Valley. She knew the ad was a stripper call, but thought I was a good-looking guy who could handle it. We just chalked it up to experience and shuffled despondently back to the car. Eventually we would laugh about it.

We arrived in Brisbane for good towards the end of 1999 and slept in the car for a few nights while we looked for a place to rent. Kristy had applied for a job working in catering at Brisbane Airport and we soon found a small apartment to let in Nundah in the city's north.

With showbiz on the backburner for the time being and still determined to improve myself, I enrolled in Hendra Secondary College to re-sit Year 12 from scratch. I wanted to graduate from high school at the proper standard, not only to boost my chances of good employment opportunities but to prove to myself and the world that I was capable of it, that I was a worthy Australian. To help pay the bills I landed a part-time job selling door-to-door Foxtel subscriptions and at sales kiosks in shopping centres. I even had a flashy title: 'Cable Adviser'.

Our domestic life ticked along nicely. It had been a long time since I'd been directed to cut up trays of meat and, although I kept having the odd nightmare about being dead, shot at and surrounded by corpses, I felt like I was a bit more settled in my heart – most of the time, anyway. I hadn't stopped growing moody and sometimes volatile if I felt cornered or threatened. But mostly I was happy, and I adored Kristy. I felt like I had a wife, so to speak, and I was grateful for the unconditional love she showed me. I enjoyed our physical relationship, too – even the kissing part.

On 17 November 2000, I completed Year 12 at Hendra Secondary College. I was almost twenty-three years old. I was extremely proud when the Queensland Board of Senior Secondary School Studies presented me with my Senior Certificate. Finally I could take my place among the new generation of educated, motivated Australians who were poised to build a great future, not only for ourselves, but also for the country.

In the long run, however, that certificate ended up doing me no good whatsoever. It certainly didn't keep me out of jail.

12

MENTAL

I was walking along the street one rainy day when a car appeared out of nowhere, ploughed through a giant puddle and sent a geyser of filthy water all over the pretty young girl who'd been walking in front of me. She was soaked from head to toe and the poor thing had been dressed all in white, too. She was rightfully shocked and annoyed but I could also see her thinking, 'How am I going to get these whites looking bright again?' Me and a couple of other pedestrians looked on thinking the same thing. 'What *is* she going to do about those stains?' The solution? Simply soak the clothes in Omo, then throw them in the wash with the rest of the load.

It was my first ever TV commercial but none of my friends and family got to see it; apparently it was only screened in Vietnam. I can't remember what I got paid to play a stunned-looking black dude behind the damsel in distress but I was happy to finally be doing a bit of extra work to supplement my income from Foxtel.

A few months after my aborted audition to be a naked beefcake I had a set of professional photos taken so I could start angling for modelling work. I had also discovered there were businesses called agencies that helped aspiring models and actors find work. I never thought I would become a star actor – not like Schwarzenegger in *Commando* – but I figured an agent could help me get some paid time in front of a camera. And they did.

'You'd be good in commercials,' I was told.

I appeared in some local TV ads and some print campaigns, too. One commercial for a new four-wheel drive took full advantage of my bona fide African appeal. I was depicted as a tribesman who was in awe of a vehicle that was so tough it had emerged from a seemingly impenetrable jungle. I was in a Just Jeans campaign, too, and I even appeared as an extra in an Australian citizenship commercial, which was fitting considering I'd proudly become an Australian citizen myself as soon as I was eligible to in 1999.

I was an extra in some movies and TV shows as well, including *Cyber Girl*, plus the live-action film of *Scooby Doo* and a horror film made for TV called *The Curse of the Talisman*. These were all small steps, but at least they were genuine footfalls along what I hoped would one day become a career path.

My ingrained Dinka work ethic meant I was always on the lookout for opportunities to get busy. Before long, Kristy and I had saved enough money to put down a deposit on a four-bedroom house in Aspley. It was on the market for $148,000 and the bank agreed to give us a loan. Kristy couldn't wait to tell her parents, but when she did, her dad cautioned that we were too young for such a major commitment and warned us against it. That missed opportunity to buy into the Australian real-estate dream also marked the beginning of the end for our relationship.

Living in Brisbane had brought me into contact with other South Sudanese refugees who had begun to arrive in the Sunshine State. I fell in with a core group of black buddies – Charles, Matthew, Michael and Joshua – plus many others who had managed to escape the war. I started hanging out with them and, while they drank alcohol and smoked a little weed, I stayed on the straight and narrow.

I had only smoked marijuana once, during my time in the rebels, and I had regretted it ever since. I would have been thirteen or fourteen when an older soldier handed me a joint. Following the lead of the other boys, I cautiously sipped a single puff of smoke into my lungs. I coughed and spluttered like an old man but a few minutes later I felt very strange: anxious, slightly removed from and yet very exposed to the world. One toke is all it took and from that moment I never quite felt the same again. I can't put my finger on it, even today, other than to say those first molecules of marijuana took something from me and I never got it back. I vowed to never smoke the stinking weed again, but that was before I began life in Australia.

Kristy's parents had split up and her mum had moved to the Gold Coast. Pretty soon, Kristy started driving down there from Nundah on the weekends to spend time with her. I'd usually tag along, but sometimes I stayed behind in Brisbane to hang out with the boys. After a while, Kristy moved to the Gold Coast permanently. I spent more time there, too, but gradually less and less of it with Kristy and her mum. A crack had opened up in our relationship and it grew wider by the day. Before long, I fell right through it.

I took the break-up hard. I moved into my own one-bedroom unit on the Gold Coast where I became a brooding mess. I was angry, grief-stricken, depressed, kind of okay and then grief-stricken again – all within a half-hour period in a cycle that repeated itself day in, day out. By any account, I was in a terrible way and I showed no signs of levelling out emotionally. Kristy was the first woman who had ever shown me love and it had a profound, powerful effect on me. When it was gone I felt like I had nothing to hold on to.

On a different level, I was always mindful that I had been given a brand-new life in a free and beautiful country. Millions of my Sudanese countrymen had died and others were still trapped or displaced by the war but for some reason I had been given a second chance and with a broken relationship I felt like I had blown it. I was certain I would never find love again.

I went from being on the verge of buying a house to thinking about the best way to kill myself frighteningly quickly. In Africa it would have been easy but with no gun available I reckoned stepping in front of a train or a speeding semi-trailer would be the best. As I languished in this fragile mental state, the recurring nightmares about death returned like an old foe that had smelled blood in the water. I could hardly get to sleep at night so, at my wits' end, I started drinking now and then, just so I could fall unconscious. Wary of the evils of drinking straight spirits, I discovered sweet-tasting pre-mixed cans of spirits called UDLs. After a while, I developed a real taste for them. And then a real need for them.

Amid the misery, however, I had flashes of something new and wonderful in my life. Her name was Mary. She was a smart, kind-hearted and beautiful brunette I dated on and off as my relationship with Kristy was coming to an end. Just as I was falling for Mary, though, we had to break it off when she moved to Sydney for work. In time, Mary – more than anyone in the world – would turn my life around. But first, I would have to go through years of hell and, tragically, I'd end up taking Mary on the doomed roller-coaster ride with me.

In the meantime, my African friends in Brisbane were always on hand to help me drown my sorrows, as were some Aussie mates I had made. Australian guys reckoned beer was the best remedy for a broken heart.

'Here, get this into you, Daniel,' they'd say and hand me a stubby of XXXX. The first time I tasted beer I nearly spat it straight back out.

'This tastes like piss,' I told them, holding up the beer like a specimen bottle. 'I mean, like *actual* piss!'

'And how would you know that, Dan?' one of them asked me.

'Because I used to be a soldier and I've had to drink my piss to survive and that's what it fucking tastes like,' I said.

'You drank your own piss?' The Australians were incredulous.

'Listen, if you're in the hot jungle all day or marching across a desert with no water, you'd drink it, too,' I assured them.

'Well, this is beer, Dan. It's the best drink in Australia so you've got a real problem.'

Of course, they had no idea how deep my problems ran. But honestly, at that time, neither did I. It was Kristy's mum who finally convinced me I needed to get some professional help to get out of the miserable hole I had found myself in. She'd gotten to know me well over the years and showed a bit of maternal fondness towards me. She organised for me to see a local GP.

'What seems to be the problem?' the doctor asked me.

'I haven't been feeling very well,' I said.

'OK, why?'

'Because I broke up with my girlfriend.'

'Really? That's it?'

'Yeah. Her mother said I should come and see you guys. I don't feel all right.'

The doctor handed me a script for some sleeping pills and gave me a referral to see a psychiatrist in a few weeks' time.

The psychiatrist's rooms were in an old Queenslander-style cottage attached to some kind of psychiatric facility near the Gold Coast Hospital. The place gave me the creeps – I could see people wandering around in gowns and other people who were dressed like security guards. It was clear to me some of the patients weren't allowed to just up and leave. It was more like a prison.

There is no sensitivity towards or understanding of mental illness in the Dinka culture. It only arouses derision, fear and insults. 'Stay away from that guy, he's *mental*.' But there I was, at a psychiatric clinic on the other side of the world, getting my mental health assessed.

The psychiatrist asked me to describe in detail what was going on. I told him I had been a child soldier and how I'd survived the war and about being a refugee. I also explained how, a year or so after coming to Australia, I had started having nightmares and flashbacks about death and dying, and how I'd hallucinated that I was stabbing members of my family. I told him how I had felt suicidal after breaking up with Kristy.

'Have you ever smoked marijuana?' the doctor asked.

'Yeah, once or twice recently,' I admitted, since I had started smoking a bit of weed with the boys as well as drinking.

After several more appointments, clinical tests and evaluations, the psychiatrist told me I was suffering from something called schizophrenia. I had no idea what that meant but I also had no reason to doubt him. After all, the guy was a doctor! He would have done really well in Year 12 and gone to university for years to learn all about schizophrenia. If he said I was schizophrenic then I was schizophrenic – no question about it.

'OK, doctor, what happens from here?'

'I'm going to put you on medication,' he said.

I went home and started taking the pills. Within two weeks I was sleeping better but I also felt mentally numb and I had no energy. I'd been an active person but I found I could barely drag myself off the couch or even move normally, like I was walking through water instead of air. Sometimes I'd have a bizarre feeling that I was someone else other than me.

Spooked, I threw the tablets into the bin after two months. It was a bad move because a day or so later I started to shake uncontrollably. Apparently it was a drug you couldn't just stop taking – you had to wean yourself off it slowly, if not stay on it forever.

As the shaking got worse I made an appointment to go back to the psychiatrist. I couldn't get there fast enough. My hands were racked by tremors as I gripped the steering wheel and when I got stuck at a set of lights on the way, I felt like my body was going to explode and paint the inside of my car a sticky red.

'Please turn green! Please turn green! Please turn green!' I pleaded.

When I finally got to the clinic I literally ran inside, where the psychiatrist prescribed me some more tablets. 'I told you not to stop taking them,' he admonished me. 'Do not stop taking these ones, under any circumstances, OK?' He handed me a new script: it was a drug called Seroquel, a stupefying anti-psychotic routinely used to treat schizophrenics.

I did what the doctor said. I ran straight to the chemist downstairs, got the pills and put one in my mouth. Soon my body stopped shaking. For the next eight years, I gobbled the pills nearly every single day for a couple of weeks on and a couple of weeks off, despite the fact that, it would eventually be shown, I never even had schizophrenia in the first place.

I had no way of knowing it but all along I had been suffering from a mentally debilitating condition called post-traumatic stress disorder (PTSD) as a result of my experiences as a boy soldier. But since nobody picked that up, it went completely untreated. Instead, I was put on the wrong drug – a particularly heavy drug – to treat a psychotic disorder I didn't have. At any rate, my life soon began to resemble a fire at a garbage dump.

Being on anti-psychotic drugs I found that I ran into other people who were on anti-psychotic drugs. This led to all kinds of pharmaceutical misbehaviour. I started hanging out with a few people who were on different kinds of medication and sometimes we'd swap pills with each other to see if we'd get a different effect. Some drugs would boost your energy and make you feel speedy while others, like the Seroquel, would just zonk you out and leave you cemented into your couch.

These same people were into illegal drugs and before long I had dabbled in ecstasy and cocaine. On top of all that I started drinking more. I also started smoking more weed. Eventually I started selling weed, too. Lots of it.

As things had been falling apart with Kristy I briefly shared a flat in Nundah with a charming, slightly crazy Aussie guy named Alan. We met one day while I was browsing through a clothing store that I liked for its great range of hip-hop street fashion that I'd taken to wearing at the time. One of the sales staff ambled over and introduced himself.

'Heyyy! How you doin', bra? What's your name?' he asked. The guy seemed friendly and funny, and he was a good salesman, too. 'My name is Alan. I work here. What do you want? I'll do a discount for you. Let's get it goin' on, man!'

He was a larrikin and I liked him straightaway. Alan offered me some style tips plus some good deals on clothes, but he was also keen to talk about his music. Maybe it's because I was a black guy but he suggested we get together some time and 'lay down some rhymes'. I may have looked the part sometimes but I was anything but a rapper – not even close. I was definitely more Bob Dylan than Biggie Smalls and the time I spent working on Queensland farms had left me with a taste for country crooners like the great Slim Dusty.

My singing career had begun with a heartfelt ode to my baby bull and ended with rousing battle songs championing the virtues of the mighty Sudanese soldier. Sadly, the war had put an end to my dreams of becoming a famous tribal songsmith, and I reckoned a hip-hop career was just as unlikely. Alan wasn't the least bit put off; I was a black man so I *must* be able to rap, right? He gave me his phone number and home address and we started hanging out. Pretty soon we were sharing the apartment together in Nundah. I kept selling Foxtel subscriptions while Alan beavered away at the shop.

Aside from rap music, Alan absolutely loved drugs. I'd sit in our lounge room after work and watch in amazement as he'd cram chopped-up weed into a little brass cone, light it on fire and suck it through a bong. With lungs full of dope, he'd tilt his head back and blow a volley of smoke rings at the ceiling like a skinny, white volcano. I started to wonder how he was financing this love affair with weed because he never seemed to run out of the stuff and, as a rap artist, he wasn't exactly Eminem.

'It's pretty easy as a matter of fact, Dan,' Alan explained. 'I can get you a bag of weed for $80 and you can sell that for $150. You can turn that $150 into $300. With the $300 you can buy a full ounce which you can make $500 to $600 out of.' This sounded more like an invitation to start doing business than it was an explanation of why he always had weed.

I knew selling drugs was illegal but I figured pot wasn't a hard, evil drug like heroin, the thought of which had always terrified me. Before long, I joined Alan in dealing pot from our unit as a sideline. It was the easiest money I had ever made.

Within a year I was living alone on the Gold Coast in a Seroquel-numbed haze. The drug was like a brain hammer and on days when I knew I'd be going to a nightclub later I wouldn't take it. Clubbing had become an escape for me since I wanted to socialise and meet new people after the break-up with Kristy. Because there weren't many black people on the Gold Coast, I was treated almost like a celebrity and sometimes I reckoned I knew how it felt to be 50 Cent.

In my spare time I'd hang out at shopping centres. One day I was sitting at Harbour Town on the Gold Coast when a well-dressed guy walked over and introduced himself.

'Hey man, whassup? I'm Will,' he said.

'Hi, I'm Dan,' I replied. 'Whassup with you?'

'I'm good. Where you from?' he asked. It was obvious to me he was intrigued by my black skin. He may have even seen me on the local nightclub circuit.

'I'm Sudanese, man,' I said.

'Oh, OK,' he said. 'I'm Lebanese.'

I couldn't help thinking there was something about the guy. He had the aura of a smooth villain in a movie and he had a gun tattooed on his arm. He said he lived at Labrador and suggested I hang out at the Grand Hotel there some time. After we chatted for a bit, he gave me his phone number and home address.

When Will looked at me he must have thought, There's something about that guy, too, because the second time I met him he was quite upfront in telling me he was a drug supplier. A big one, who specialised in ecstasy.

Soon I was buying a few pills from Will, here and there. Then I started buying bigger quantities and he gradually introduced me to a network of Gold Coast drug barons. Some moved pills and powders while others dealt in weed. I became a customer to a few of them, buying moderate amounts of pot in order to rekindle my own start-up drug business. Although I had only wanted to sell enough to keep me in my own supply it was soon my main source of income. Before anyone knew it, I had transformed into a drug dealer.

I had a growing dependence on marijuana and a gallop-ing thirst for alcohol to help wash down the daily dose of Seroquel. I had convinced myself this unholy chemical trinity helped me relax and tune out the problems of the world. In reality, they just temporarily blotted them out and compounded my issues even more as I messed around with my brain cells. It wasn't what the doctor had ordered.

13

SUPRA MAN

As a low-level drug dealer I had an oversupply of something I'd gone without most of my life: money. With no concept of what to do with it all I blew most of it drinking, gambling and partying away in Gold Coast nightclubs. Sadly, that was what my ambitions had shrunk to. Instead of pursuing my goal of working in TV and film, I found myself associating with some shady characters into the small, dirty hours of the morning.

Unsurprisingly, I started to attract the attention of police. From the time I was medicated for schizophrenia in 2002 I morphed from a quiet citizen who'd never had a parking ticket into a small-time crook. I had a criminal record ranging from disorderly conduct and breaching bail to more serious offences including drink-driving, common assault and obstructing police. I found myself in front of Southport Magistrates Court no fewer than ten times in two years. Some charges were thrown out but others were proven and I was either fined, let off with a warning, sentenced to community service or placed on probation.

I wasn't always blameless and I made plenty of mistakes, but trouble also had a way of finding me. A lot of my brushes with the law arose after I was racially abused or outright attacked. Being a reasonably tall black guy I attracted unwanted attention from people wanting to show off or prove themselves. Plenty of guys went out of their way to pick fights with me.

I truly hated violence. I had seen far too much of it and I knew that when human beings let loose they were capable of the most heinous acts. I wasn't so righteous as to think I was any exception and I was terrified of what damage I might end up doing if I was overtaken by the rush of blood that can turn humans into panicking animals.

Where I came from, fighting wasn't simply an exchange of punches until someone fell down. In Sudan we fought like lions – all the way until one of the parties didn't get back up. With the exception of my boyhood torturer Anyang and the drunken rebel who had murdered my brother, I never wanted to hurt anybody like that. Still, people kept coming at me in Australia.

I was out on the town one night when a Kiwi guy called me a black cunt and spat at me. I wrestled him onto the footpath and slammed his head repeatedly into the gutter. He was OK but I felt bad that I had been like a lion – not completely in control. Another night, someone relentlessly taunted me and called me a 'filthy ape' so I threw a bottle at his head. It grazed the top of his skull but had it been a direct hit it would have knocked him out, or worse. There were countless other times when I was either king-hit in the street, abused or spat on when I opted to walk away instead, scared that the big cat in me might leap out and do something everyone regretted.

One night I was knocked out cold after a couple of burly security guards refused me entry to a Gold Coast nightclub. It was early in the evening; I was polite and hadn't even had a drink yet so I could see no reason for them not to let me in along with the rest of Surfers Paradise, who were all lining up at the door – other than the fact I was a 'fucking nigger'.

'Hold it there, buddy. You're not going in,' one of the guards told me, shoving a palm into my chest.

'Huh? Why not?' I wanted to know.

'You're just not fucking going in, mate, so fuck off before you regret it.'

Apparently another black man had caused a ruckus there the previous week and since we apparently 'all look the same' I was now paying for his crimes. That sort of thing happened a lot, not just to me but to many of my African friends.

'It wasn't me, man, you've got everything mixed up,' I protested.

That's when I heard a voice in the crowd nearby let rip with the f-word and the n-word.

'Yeah, r-i-i-ight,' I said, turning back to the security guards. 'You guys are just bloody racist, aren't you?'

They grabbed me, dragged me a few metres and threw

me hard to the ground behind a brick wall, where they beat me to a pulp. An ambulance was called to take me to hospital, but when the police investigated, the nightclub's CCTV footage only showed one of my legs protruding from behind the wall and no evidence of anything untoward – no swinging fists and stomping boots, no torn and blood-spattered shirt hanging off me and no swollen, bleeding head. When it came to bashing fucking niggers, those bouncers had it to down to a fine art. With no other corroborating evidence, no charges were laid.

They weren't the only tough guys I brushed up against on the Gold Coast nightclub circuit. Over time, I became acquainted with a pair of handsome young brothers named Dionne and Jade Lacey – names that would one day become infamous in Queensland's underworld circles.

Jade and Dionne were the sons of a former Victorian milk-run owner named Ken Lacey, who had turned his little business into a multimillion-dollar dairy distribution empire before retiring to live the good life in the Sunshine State. Dionne and Jade didn't appear to share their dad's work ethic. They preferred to cruise the streets in flashy BMWs, deck themselves out in designer clothes, party in glitzy bars and finance the whole show by running a large-scale drug-supply business. I happened to be one of their early customers.

For a time, I would purchase bulk orders of ecstasy from Dionne and Jade. If I bought three hundred pills from them for $10 each I'd on-sell them for $20 and turn $3000 into $6000 with virtually no effort required. On the surface it all seemed so easy, and part of me felt like I was living the good life. But I had entered a seedy and dangerous underworld. Although I didn't realise it at the time, the stakes were extremely high.

While I personally never had any problems with the Lacey boys, others did. A year or so after I first met them, I learned from watching the TV that Jade and Dionne abducted an associate they claimed had ripped them off in a drug deal. The brothers took the terrified young man on a midnight boat ride at gunpoint to an island just off the coast, where they forced him to dig his own grave by moonlight. In the end they only shot the poor guy in the hand and eventually let him go. Their next victim wasn't so lucky.

In 2007 the Lacey boys were jailed over the shooting death of another associate in another drug deal gone wrong. Eleven years after that, their father Ken was also sent to prison after he was caught with a large stash of cocaine in his apartment. The former milkman reckoned the downfall of his sons led to his own life running off the rails.

I struggled to make sense of the demise of such a successful and lucky family. As far as I could see, Dionne and Jade had been born with golden tickets in life and they simply tore them up and threw them away. As the sons of a multimillionaire, they had been given opportunities others could only dream of.

Their upbringing was about as far as you could get from my early days foraging for food on a garbage dump in Juba or sleeping among cows in Twic. But were they happy like

I had been? Did all that money make their lives better than mine? Obviously not. Had my childhood not been interrupted by a war I can honestly say I'd have preferred the simple tribal life to Dionne and Jade's white-knuckle existence in the West. And yet, there I was in their concrete jungle dealing drugs too, so who was I to judge?

The laws of supply and demand dictated that I made vastly more money than I required to simply feed my own habit. I had trouble spending it all and ended up giving a lot of it away. In 2003 my mum had been granted refugee status and came to live in Australia, settling in Toowoomba with the rest of the family. The day she arrived at Brisbane Airport the whole family was there to greet her. John Riedel, the amazing man who had bankrolled much of my early phone contact with Mum, came along to welcome her to Australia, too. When I wrapped her in my arms in the arrivals hall I couldn't find the words to express my feelings. I just clung to my mother and wept like a baby.

Of course, she didn't know about my secret life. There's no way I would have dared give Mum money that was made illegally, especially through selling drugs; it would have gone against everything she believed in. So with Mum safely in Australia, I splurged on friends and even strangers instead.

It was nothing for me to drive up to Brisbane or Toowoomba with my car loaded full of alcohol to share with all of my buddies. As a burgeoning alcoholic, I'd drink booze for the entire journey. I'd travel with cases of UDL cans, cases full of premixed Jim Beam and cola, and bottles of all kinds of spirits piled on the seats. These would be handed out at parties or just for the hell of it.

In the nightclubs it was perpetually my shout and it wasn't uncommon for me to spend $1500 to $2000 a night buying top-shelf drinks for my friends like Michael and Matthew, and even for complete strangers. My pockets were always full of cash. If I saw little African kids at the basketball courts in Brisbane I'd hand them $20 each.

I spent money on myself, too. My biggest blow-out at that point had been a whopping $36,000 on my pride and joy – a black 1997 Toyota Supra Turbo sports car. I first laid eyes on one when I went to see *The Fast and the Furious* at the cinema in 2001 and I knew I just had to get one. I used some of the money I'd earned legally when saving for the house in Aspley and got finance for the balance. When the drug money started flowing in, it wasn't long before I owned the car outright. That I didn't end up dying in the thing is truly a miracle.

Now I was a serial drink-driver, I had graduated from just being a garden-variety revhead to a menace on the roads. These days I own a gutless little hatchback and I drive it like an old man. But in the early noughties, in a downward drug spiral that started after I was misdiagnosed and wrongly prescribed medication, I was out of control.

I give thanks to God that I never hurt or killed anyone, myself included. I have a lot to be ashamed about during what I would come to see as my 'lost years', and my driving record is right up there with the things I wish I could do over.

Back then, though, I loved nothing more than racing other revheads in sports cars, especially along the M1 Pacific Motorway that links the Gold Coast with Brisbane. I would always be on the lookout for other speed machines of renown – Nissan Skylines, Subaru WRXs, Ford XR8s – and once I'd lock eyes with the drivers we'd treat the M1 as our own personal racetrack.

I had a few friends who also owned nice cars, and we'd sometimes drive along the M1 as a screeching, weaving convoy of hoons. Not only would I tip UDLs and Jim Beam down my throat during these expeditions, I'd smoke bongs at the steering wheel. Once, a bunch of us even drove to Brisbane passing a bong back and forth out our windows, from speeding car to speeding car.

The weather in south-east Queensland was always great and often hot, so I'd cruise around the Gold Coast in my Supra with my shirt off: a shiny black man in his shiny black sports car making a shiny spectacle of himself. I was one of those idiots who'd rev the engine at traffic lights and drop the clutch as soon as the signal turned green. The tyres would smoke and the car would fishtail up the street, and I'd sit there bare-chested behind the wheel as if I were starring in *The Fast and the Furious: Surfers Paradise*.

It's a wonder I never ended up starring in the 6 pm news as the latest statistic in the national road toll. Once I was driving drunk behind one of my maniac friends along a two-lane stretch of highway west of Toowoomba when he pulled into the oncoming lane and overtook seven or eight cars in one go. Naturally I took this as a challenge and when I saw a break in the oncoming traffic I pulled out to the right, dropped the Supra back into third gear and hit the gas like I was on Mt Panorama in Bathurst. As I shifted up into fourth gear, then fifth, I passed a lot of cars, but I was also headed straight at an eighteen-wheeler loaded with live pigs that was coming the other way.

The horrified truck driver blasted his horn in desperation and, just as I passed the tenth car, I managed to fling the Supra back into the left-hand lane with millimetres between me and instant death. I could have killed people right then and there and I still shudder when I think about that split second and those precious millimetres. But on the day I just settled the adrenaline by reaching for another can of UDL.

Obviously, the Supra and I were destined to run out of luck.

—

More and more refugees from the war in Sudan were granted asylum in Australia. Many settled in south-east Queensland like our family had done, while others were taken to start new lives in Melbourne.

For the most part, I preferred to hang out with white Australians rather than spending all my time with people I shared a birthplace with. This was mainly because I'd fallen in love with the Australian sense of humour. A lot of black guys tended to be wound up pretty tight, whereas I found Aussies more inclined to laugh at a tricky situation rather than take offence at it. Still, I had my tight group of three close Sudanese friends: Charles, Matthew and Michael.

Charles was one of my best friends in Australia. Like the others, I met him through the Dinka community in Brisbane and we hit it off straightaway. Charles was younger than me; a quiet guy with a beautiful smile who came off a bit like an African American gangsta with bandanas and low-slung pants. He was also a nutcase behind the wheel – another thing we shared. After living for a while in Brisbane, his parents decided to move down to Melbourne and Charles went with them.

One night a few months after he'd gone, I was at a party at some white people's house on the Gold Coast with Matthew, Michael, Michael's nephew Joshua, and a Croatian friend named Ivan. As usual, I was drunk, and when I noticed one of the Australian girls at the party was crying I asked her what had happened. She told me one of the white guys had slapped her across the face. Outraged, I confronted him and a fight erupted. Just as it was getting out of hand, my phone rang inside my pocket. It was a Melbourne number and the person on the other end said, 'I'm sorry to tell you that Charles is dead. He was killed in a car accident.'

I was devastated by the horrible news that had just turned up in my pocket from out of nowhere. I stood there in a state of shock while punches were still being traded, then I decided on the spot that we had to drive to Melbourne immediately. I'd left the Supra at home that night and had instead driven to the party in an old Ford Laser I'd picked up as a general runabout. We all piled into the car and it wasn't until we had fled the party/fight that I told everyone else about Charles. But before anyone had any time to react, I was pulled over by an RBT unit.

Ivan was the only sober one in the car and he happened to be in the passenger seat. 'Quick, let's switch seats,' I said.

'OK,' he said, shimmying into the driver's seat as I squeezed my big frame over the top of him. 'But I think the police already saw you.'

Of course they had. 'Everything is being recorded, sir,' the officer said as he pointed at me through the window. '*You* were driving.' Instead of heading to Melbourne to grieve for my lost friend I was taken to the Southport Watchhouse and charged with drink-driving. Not that this setback stopped me from making a series of appalling decisions that put my life and the lives of others at risk; it just postponed the process temporarily.

As soon as I was released from the police cells in the morning we returned to get the Laser from the scene of the previous night's RBT stop, only to find its windows had all been smashed in. It seemed the Aussies had the last say in the fight after all. We went straight home, grabbed the Supra and the next thing we knew Matthew, Michael, Joshua and I were hurtling down the Pacific Highway in a car crammed full of alcohol.

Matthew and I shared the drink-driving and it took us just eighteen hours to travel the nearly eighteen hundred kilometres to the southern capital. The only reason we stopped along the way was to refuel or to pee beside the road.

Somehow we made it to Melbourne alive and spent two days in a drunken stupor, mourning Charles and weeping as his coffin was lowered into the ground. We then re-stocked the Supra with a booty of Jim Beam cans, climbed aboard like a haunted gang of drunken pirates and set sail back to Queensland.

Along the way, one of the boys convinced me to stop in Sydney because he wanted to see a friend. It was my first ever trip to the harbour city but the closest we got to water was a tap at some basketball courts in Sydney's sprawling western suburbs. There, we managed to get ourselves in another fight because we were still drunk and highly emotional about Charles. All it took was one wrong word here or one wrong look there and we were set to explode. One of the Sydney people pulled a knife and threatened Joshua so we dived back into the Supra and fishtailed out of there.

On the way out of Sydney we stopped at a convenience store so Joshua could buy a packet of cigarettes. While we were waiting around inside I picked up a pair of sunglasses from one of the rotating carousels and tried them on.

Yeah, man, they look good, I thought as I checked myself out in the little mirror on top of the display. Then I slipped them straight into my pocket.

'PUT THEM BACK BEFORE I SHOOT YOU!' the shopkeeper boomed at the top of his lungs.

I never saw a gun but Joshua started pleading with the guy. 'Don't shoot! Don't shoot! He's not a thief! He's just drunk and being stupid. He has money to pay with. Just don't shoot him!'

I put the sunglasses back and we left without any bullet wounds.

Next it was my turn to call for a detour – a big one. My sister Aguil had moved to Canberra and, since I'd spent the past few days driving drunk through half the states of Australia, I thought an impromptu visit from me and my shitfaced friends was just what she needed.

As before, we only stopped for fuel or when we needed to piss by the roadside, which was plenty, given the amount of grog we were drinking. It was dark by the time we left Sydney and during our next toilet stop I was struck on the hip by a passing car. The impact spun me around like a top and nearly knocked me off my feet. I heard something clattering along the roadway. I was so drunk I hardly felt any pain but when the car that had hit me came back they were shocked and relieved to see me still standing.

'Are you all right? Oh my God I just didn't see you!' the driver gasped. He would have been doing at least a hundred kilometres per hour when he hit me.

'Nah-nah-nah-nah . . . I'm OK,' I slurred. 'I can walk. I'm fine.'

That's when the driver noticed his passenger-side mirror was missing – obviously the item I'd heard bouncing down the highway. The smallest of grazes on my hip showed where the thing had barely clipped me. Had I been a few centimetres more to the right I might have suffered terrible injuries or even been killed. But I *still* wasn't done dicing with death. Within an hour we stopped to have another piss and that time a speeding truck missed me by a whisker.

Unsurprisingly, Aguil wasn't exactly thrilled when four drunk Africans arrived on her doorstep. After a few hours' sleep we got up early the next morning and drove all the way back to the Gold Coast – drunk the whole way.

After Charles died, my alcohol abuse got even worse. I missed him terribly. He'd been among my closest friends and I couldn't believe he was gone. It didn't occur to me until much later just how close I'd come to joining him in the afterlife during that insane road trip to his funeral. Maybe deep down in my soul I had wanted to.

The first time I crashed the Supra into a power pole it cost me $7000 in repairs. The second time I totalled the thing it cost me a lot more than just money. I was at home on the Gold Coast, drunk and stoned as usual. Matthew, Michael and some of my white friends were there hanging out and when I got a phone call from a girl I knew inviting me over to her place I was up in a flash. Knowing I was completely off my face, Matthew had the good sense to hide the keys to my car. He was obviously trying to protect me from myself, not to mention preserve the safety of the wider community. But I didn't see it that way.

'Matthew, where are my keys, man?' I demanded.

'Oh, are you going somewhere?' he responded. 'I don't know where I put them. They're around here somewhere.'

'Matthew, man – c'mon. Give me my fucking keys!'

'Calm down, D. I don't know where your keys are, OK?'

I hit the roof and grabbed a knife from the kitchen. 'GIVE ME MY FUCKING KEYS NOW!' I screamed and stabbed the couch next to Matthew. Before I could do anything worse I remembered I had a spare key stashed in my bedroom.

'Fuck you, Matthew. Seeya later,' I said as I slammed the door behind me and stumbled to the car. I took off at high speed and made it maybe three hundred metres down the road before I lost control and crashed my beloved Supra into a steep grass embankment outside the local school. The explosion of metal brought all the neighbours out and I asked them for help to push the crumpled sports car back onto the road so I could be on my way. They checked that I was OK and told me the ambulance had already been called. The cops were right behind them, too. I was again taken to the Watchhouse and charged with a batch of offences including yet another count of DUI. But when I woke up in the police cells the next morning I couldn't remember any of it.

'Where's your pride and joy now, Mr Chut?' one of the officers asked me with a smirk.

'I don't know,' I replied, confused. 'Probably at home.'

'No,' he said. 'It's at the wrecker's.'

'Nah, it can't be,' I said, still drawing a blank on the previous night.

'You crashed it, you fucking idiot,' the cop informed me.

'No, officer. That's not possible,' I said, honestly bewildered.

'You fucking did. We've got photos here, we've got witnesses and statements and your car has been taken to the wreckers. You're lucky you didn't kill someone, you bloody maniac.'

In hindsight, being permanently separated from that vehicle was a blessing from heaven. Had we stayed together I could well have ended up killing myself or going to jail for maiming or killing innocent people – a guilt I don't think I could have lived with. I'd bought the Supra for $36,000 and spent another $7000 repairing it from my first prang so, in my mind, it had been a $43,000 car. Easy come, easy go. And I had my driver's licence revoked for more than a year.

My drinking and egregious driving weren't the only things that had got way out of control. I was more frequently swapping Seroquel with people who were on other types of heavy prescription medication. On top of all the marijuana, the results were pretty mind-scrambling. From time to time I'd wonder when the Seroquel was going to work and when I would stop being a schizophrenic. I really missed the old Ayik and I wondered if I would ever see him again.

14

BATTLE CALL

When Prime Minister John Howard sent Australian forces to join George W. Bush's 'coalition of the willing' in the 2003 invasion of Iraq, many Aussies were so outraged they protested in the streets. Not me – I was right behind Howard and desperate to join in the fight myself.

I had been raised to hate all Arabs. In my mind, they were the reason many of my friends and loved ones were dead, the reason my country was at war and the reason I'd had to endure the anguish of being a child soldier. When I was a boy, the Arabs in northern Sudan controlled everything and treated my people as not much more than slaves. Blacks were almost always limited to menial jobs or being servants to the Muslim ruling class. After I was bombed in Kapoeta, I was told the planes that dropped the ordnance had come from Iraq. So when Howard committed Aussie troops to the overthrow of

Saddam Hussein, I wanted in. A few days later, I called the Australian Defence Force.

'Hello. I'm a former child soldier and I know how to fight. How do I join the Australian Army?' I said to the woman on the other end.

I had given it a lot of thought and it seemed like a good idea. After all, I was not very well educated and was struggling to find my path in life. One thing I had experience in was soldiering so I figured the Australian Army would be a good fit. Since I was a combat veteran, I knew I had something to offer. Oddly, for a person who had fled a war zone, I also felt the same strong pull towards armed conflict as when I was compelled to join the Red Army. Surely the Aussies would be happy to have me.

'Yes, my name is Ayik Chut but they call me Daniel,' I explained to the bemused woman at the ADF. 'I fought in the war in Sudan and I can help. I'll help kill Saddam. I'll go there tomorrow.'

Needless to say, the ADF didn't take me up on my offer.

Since I wouldn't be heading to the Middle East to fight, I decided to turn my old Ford Laser hatch into a billboard to support our troops instead. I bought some white paint and daubed the back window and side doors with slogans in giant letters: SADDAM MUST GO and DOWN WITH SADDAM. Whenever I pulled up at traffic lights I attracted all kinds of looks. Some people gave me the thumbs up, some just shook their heads, while plenty of others looked scared of the black man glowering from behind the wheel of a mobile advertisement for war. I can imagine what they must have been thinking: 'Stay away from that guy. He's *mental*.'

Maybe I was. I had certainly changed dramatically since I first sought medical help. I was plagued by an underlying feeling of disquiet; I didn't feel like I was me any more. My past trauma, the break-up with Kristy, the misdiagnosis, the medication and my sense of failure despite my best efforts to succeed had all taken the wind out of my sails.

Numbed by Seroquel I found myself taking the easiest options, whether they were legal or not. Within a very short time, the conscientious young man who'd dreamed of being a doctor like his dad seemed lost to the world and an irresponsible, drugged-out, volatile, risk-taking, emotional basket case had taken his place.

Again I was back in front of Southport Magistrates Court on a DUI charge. There was an ominous feeling that I might be heading to jail this time so Aguil, Mum and two of my cousins travelled down from Toowoomba to support me. After listening to the duty solicitor's summary of my fractured life, the magistrate decided to spare me from a custodial sentence. It was quite a relief. I had been dreading going to jail so much that I downed a bunch of mystery pills that morning in a half-hearted suicide attempt. The only result was that I was a drooling, half-conscious mess in front of the court.

After I was released and put on probation, Aguil took me straight to meet a contractor she knew named Steven, who said he could give me some work. Keeping busy with a proper job might help me stay me out of trouble, Aguil had said. I liked the idea of getting back into hard, honest work. After all, it was in my Dinka blood.

Steven ran a Southport tiling business and we worked in some enormous mansions in the Gold Coast's glitziest neighbourhoods like Sovereign Islands and Runaway Bay. With a filthy rich clientele, Steven was quoting huge sums on each job – $10,000, $15,000, $20,000 – but he was paying me peanuts to lay tiles – a few hundred dollars here and there. Sometimes he didn't bother paying me at all.

'Steven, you have to pay me, man. I have done the work and you owe me money!' I complained.

'Yeah, yeah. You'll get your money,' he assured me.

I'd stay over at Steven's place sometimes, which only made the tension worse. Weeks passed and I still didn't get the money I was owed – not that I necessarily needed it, as I was still making the odd deal of weed after hours. But it was a matter of principle. The guy was ripping me off. Finally, I went to his place one day to confront him. He wasn't there so I grabbed his laptop computer, snapped it in half and ripped its electronic guts out. It was illegal and wrong, and it was also pretty stupid, considering I was on probation over the latest DUI charge. When the police arrested me I was once more taken to the Southport Watchhouse and locked up overnight.

When I fronted the magistrate the following morning his goodwill had entirely run out and I was remanded in custody for three months. Ultimately, I was convicted of wilful damage over the smashed laptop, sentenced to three months in prison, which by that time I had already served, and released.

—

Brisbane's Arthur Gorrie Correctional Centre had a reputation as being one of Australia's toughest jails. After all I had been through in Africa, I was devastated about where I had ended up. Being diagnosed as mentally ill was one thing, but to have turned into a drug dealer and now a jailbird had never been part of my life plan.

I was nervous when I arrived at prison. I was told to strip naked and wash in front of the officers with a special soap before I was de-loused, handed some prison clothes and assigned a cell. After a day or two, I was slightly relieved to find that most of the other inmates treated me pretty well.

Unlike my first day at school when all I could muster was 'Me Daniel' and 'Me child soldier', I was by now pretty good at communicating with Australian men. These new ones wanted to know my story: 'G'day mate. Watchaname? Wotcha in for?'

I explained how I'd smashed up my boss's computer because he owed me money and wouldn't pay. Not a terribly impressive charge from a criminal point of view. It certainly wasn't a marquee offence among the guests at Arthur Gorrie.

'Oh yeah?' one of the inmates drawled, then he started pointing to the other men in the exercise yard. 'Well, that guy over there is in for murder. And that bloke stabbed a guy to death.' The prison was even home to the man who was once Australia's most wanted criminal, the notorious bank robber and escape artist Brenden Abbott. Abbott was known as 'the postcard bandit' because he liked to send the police photos of himself swimming, drinking cocktails and generally living it up while on the run.

The news came as a massive shock. I thought all the murderers and rapists would be kept in a separate jail. How had it come to this? I didn't belong in there with those evil criminals! As soon as I got the opportunity I phoned the solicitor who'd represented me in court but I only got as far as the girl at reception.

'Oh my God! You've put me in with murderers!' I wailed into the phone. 'There are killers and child rapists in here! I'm not like that! Why am I in jail with killers?'

Her mystified response was something along the lines of, 'What did you expect?'

'But I'm not a murderer! I never killed anyone,' I complained. 'Why did I get put in a jail for criminals? I'm not a criminal! Not a real one.'

The court, naturally, had taken a different view. No matter how unjust I thought it, I was indeed a criminal who was being held in custody for a criminal act. If the court decided I should spend it with Australia's most wanted man and a bunch of killers, then that was that.

After a while I calmed down and realised a lot of the inmates were pretty reasonable people who, like me, just wanted to quietly do their time, pay for their mistakes and re-join the community. And for once, I wasn't the only black Sudanese in the place.

I was introduced to an inmate everyone called Africa. He, too, had come to Australia as a refugee. Africa was Nuer – the Dinka people's mortal enemy – but now that we were locked up together half a world away from Sudan, ancient animosities vanished into thin air. Africa had virtually no English and apparently he was having problems with depression.

'It'll be good for him to have you here, Daniel,' one of the inmates told me. 'His English is shit, so you might be able to help him.'

Africa's was a long, dark story. We communicated in Arabic and he told me he'd also been a child soldier. Like me, he'd been haunted by it and told me the story of the day he'd cut someone's arm off with a machete and how they bled to death. After just a few months in Australia he'd been charged with a serious offence involving violence and he was now looking down the barrel of a very long sentence. He denied the accusation and was trying to fight the charges so whenever he needed to speak to his lawyer I helped translate.

I became friendly with a few of the other inmates, too. For some reason, members of the Finks bikie gang took me under their wings and protected me from the problems that can arise in jail. I had support from outside the prison, too. My old schoolteacher and mentor John Riedel came to visit and lend an emotional shoulder to lean on. And, much to my surprise – and delight – so did Mary, the beautiful brunette I had been dating in Brisbane before she'd moved to Sydney.

Mary had called me out of the blue one day not long before I was arrested for smashing Steven's computer.

'Oh, hey, Mary – how are you going?' I gushed into the phone, surprised but genuinely glad to hear her voice.

'I'm good, Daniel,' she said. 'I'm still in Sydney.'

We chatted for a while and the next thing we knew, we were making plans for her to visit me on the Gold Coast the following week. Mary had been due to fly up to Coolangatta on the Friday but, as fate would have it, I was arrested on the Thursday. Since I was locked up, I had no way of reaching her.

As soon as Mary checked into her motel room in Surfers Paradise she tried to call me but there was no answer. She kept trying for days and still couldn't raise me. Eventually she grew worried that something bad had happened to me so before she was due to fly back to Sydney on Sunday evening she phoned the police to say the friend she'd been due to meet was missing.

'Ayik Chut?' the officer said, checking the name she'd given him. 'Ah yep, we've got him in custody, actually. Doesn't look like he's going to be getting out any time soon, I'm afraid.'

About a week later, I received a phone call at the prison. It was Mary.

'Oh my God, I'm so sorry,' I said, almost tripping over myself in the rush to explain what I'd done to end up in jail and how I had no way of contacting her to let her know.

Mary told me not to worry and promised to fly back up to Queensland the following weekend to visit me.

Over the next three months, Mary regularly visited me when I was in prison, flying up on Friday nights after work and spending the weekend visiting me in jail. She even put money into my jail account so I could buy small comforts like chocolate from the prison canteen. There's a saying that goes, 'The people who love you are the ones who visit you in jail.' My family were anxious to see me and support me but I told them all to keep away, even Mum. I didn't want them to see me locked up. There was no stopping Mary, though. Her kindness and generosity blew me away and I fell head over heels in love with her all over again.

In the end, my time inside Arthur Gorrie Correctional Centre was pretty uneventful. I went to church on Sundays and made myself a wallet in leatherwork class. Otherwise I just kept to myself and let the time slide past me. I was still taking my doses of Seroquel to keep my 'schizophrenia' under control and the brain-deadening effects were conducive to just sitting around numbly and doing nothing. I didn't find jail to be a scary environment, although some found it harder than others. Africa was one inmate who seemed to struggle with incarceration. He'd gotten mixed up in a few fights and one night he tried to kill himself.

After we'd been locked in for the night, Africa gathered together all his bedding, clothes and his mattress – anything flammable – and set it all on fire with a cigarette lighter. Immediately he started screaming and begging for help. A fire alarm had also activated, which sent guards thundering into the cellblock to let him out of his smoke-filled cage.

'Man, what were you trying to do?' I asked him in Arabic a couple of days later.

'I was trying to kill myself!' Africa replied.

That didn't make any sense to me. 'Then why the fuck did you cry out for help? You should have just choked to death. You didn't really want to die.'

'I didn't know it was going to be so bad to die like that,' he responded.

'Well, death is not easy,' I said. 'Especially when you are breathing smoke in and suffocating, you know? The only good death you can ever have is a gunshot, because it's so quick. Ten or thirty seconds of pain and then you're just dead. Gone. All over.'

Africa nodded in agreement. 'The only problem with that, Ayik,' he explained, 'is they won't let us keep guns in our cells.'

15

DEAD MAN WALKING

After we somehow rekindled our relationship in the drab surrounds of a maximum-security prison, Mary left her job in Sydney and moved to Queensland. We lived with a friend of a friend, then we found a place in Southport and my old friend Michael rented the spare room. I could not believe I suddenly had Mary back in my life. She had always reminded me of the American singer Taylor Swift: slender, delicately pretty and strongly magnetic. As a human being she was loyal, loving, funny, warm, considerate and smart. She was also now a little older and a little wiser. There had been a lot of changes during the years we'd been apart – mostly to do with me.

For starters, the new Ayik was a clinically diagnosed schizophrenic who tipped a jumble of powerful brain drugs into his mouth every day. He was also a heavy binge-drinker at best and a raging alcoholic at worst. As a dope-smoker he would have put the most committed Rastafarian to shame, and last but not least he'd traded in his job as a model and dreams of working in movies for life as a suburban drug dealer.

In truth, I kept my criminal life secret from Mary. She'd landed a job in administration and as soon as she'd leave the house each day I would set about my usual business selling weed. My time in prison hardly put a dent in my operation. A few weeks after my release, word spread among the Gold Coast potheads that I was back in business. My parole required me to attend drug and alcohol treatment programs and I was still seeing my psychiatrist every few weeks to monitor my schizophrenia, but none of it stopped me from doing exactly what I wanted. Mary thought I smoked a little pot here and there but she had no idea how much of a fiend I had become. If she suspected I was selling pot, too, she would have been shocked by the true scale of it.

As with almost everybody else in my life, I also kept Mary largely in the dark about the problems that constantly cartwheeled through my head. I had deliberately built a wall between her and my childhood trauma. I rarely said a word about the war and if I ever did mention it in passing I would completely shut down if Mary gently tried to ask me anything more about it. I was hardly laying the foundations of a solid relationship.

Mary was no dummy; she could see I had problems, so she sometimes kept me at arm's length, too. Her mum still lived in Brisbane so Mary would spend a fair bit of time up there and then come down to the Gold Coast to stay with me from time to time. Of course, that meant Michael and I often had the townhouse to ourselves, which made it easier to conceal my nefarious activities from Mary.

Although dealing drugs definitely made me a criminal and while I think back on it with immense shame today, at the time I didn't feel like one. I considered it more like cutting corners. The way my screwed-up mind saw things, I wasn't a *criminal's* criminal, not like the Lacey brothers. I had no desire to carry a gun around or make people dig their own graves. Hell, I wasn't even concerned about making piles of money, let alone enforcing debt collection. I sold drugs because it was the easiest way I could provide for my own habit. Also, it was quite possibly one of the only things I was capable of doing at that point of my life.

I had trouble holding down regular jobs. I had tried on a few occasions, but they never lasted. That's not to say that drinking heavily and smoking pot helped me pull myself out of the dive I had spiralled into. Once I'd dragged myself out of bed in the morning I would flop straight back down onto the couch in front of the TV.

Since I smoked a lot of pot I grew quite paranoid about the amount of 'visitors' I would receive. I had slowly built up a regular and loyal clientele so there were usually quite a few customers to deal with on any given day. In an effort to make the revolving door nature of the enterprise look less suspicious, I wouldn't let my customers simply pick up a deal and go; I told them to stick around for a while, like regular friends might, and smoke a few cones with me. Whenever there was a knock at the door I'd turn into the consummate host. 'Oh hey! Good to seeya, my man! Come on in. Sit down and relax. How's your day going? Here, have a smoke.'

Since I was Southport's most gregarious drug dealer and not motivated by traditional criminal greed, I tended to give out extremely generous deals. Not only would my customers leave the townhouse with more than their money's worth in drugs, they'd shuffle out of the place stoned off their heads on the complimentary pot I'd given them. No suspicious activity at all!

The townhouse was in a large, low-rise complex of more than one hundred residences that were accessible via a network of little driveways and paths. There were a number of ways you could leave my place so, even though there were quite a few people coming and going, the operation wasn't as obvious as it might otherwise have been. I was also kept fairly busy answering any one of my three phones. People would ring to a) make sure I was at home and b) make sure I had product, or 'chicken' as I had instructed them to call it over the phone. Chicken was marijuana.

'Yeah hello, D? How you goin', man? I just thought I might pop over and pick up some chicken,' a typical phone conversation might begin.

'No worries, man,' I'd reply chirpily. 'Come over.'

'Yeah no worries, man. Seeya in a bit.'

Like that wasn't suspicious either! I was always fearful of being busted and I constantly sprinkled pepper all over the front and back landings of the townhouse in an effort to throw sniffer dogs off the trail. I'd heard that once dogs got a snoutful of nice, fine pepper they start sneezing all over the place. This was supposed to totally mess with their sense of smell and render their drug-detecting abilities void. But no amount of doorstep seasoning was going to stop the drug squad from paying me a visit.

When they finally turned up it was at four o'clock in the morning. *Bom-bom-bom-bom-bom* on the door.

'Huh, what?' I was half asleep and very confused.

Bom-bom-bom-bom-bom on the door again. Both doors actually, front and back.

'Police! Open up. We have a warrant to search these premises.'

The next thing I knew the townhouse was full of cops, plus a police dog that didn't appear to be having any kind of sneezing fit. There was just me and one of my Aussie mates, an ex-country boy named Nick, in the house. The previous day we'd been due to go out and score a couple of pounds of marijuana from a higher-level drug supplier but the deal had fallen through. Nick had ended up staying over for the night and smoking a few bongs with what little pot we had left.

After a thorough search of the place all the police could find was the bong, which happened to be Nick's so he took the blame for it. They had absolutely nothing on me. Funnily enough, the sniffer dog missed the three hundred ecstasy pills I had hidden under the carpet on the stairs. As far as the police were concerned, I was in the clear.

It was the luckiest break I had ever caught and perhaps the unluckiest day of their careers.

After that, the police never bothered coming back, and that's when things *really* got out of hand. Had the drug squad returned six months or a year later they would have hit the jackpot and I would've been going to jail for a long time. It was not uncommon for me to have two pounds of dope at the townhouse – minimum. At one point, I was sitting on twelve pounds with a wholesale value of $30,000 to $40,000 and a street value of God knows how much.

I could usually buy a pound for $2500 to $2600. Generally, I could turn that investment into $3500. Of course, this required me to do business with upper-level drug suppliers – heavy criminals who faced serious jail time if they were ever caught, so people like me had to slowly earn their trust. Once I did, I got a glimpse inside their world.

There was one guy I bought large quantities off who would keep highly compressed pounds of dope worth upwards of $100,000 in his home. These weren't like green garbage bags filled with loosely packed, pungent-smelling buds – they were dense, tightly wrapped, inch-thick bricks of product that looked like they'd come from a factory. You couldn't even smell that it was dope, which usually reeks. This guy had a bathtub full of them with a pile of dirty laundry on top and his kids running around like it was a normal family situation. When I'd get it home and open one of the bricks, the stink of cannabis was almost overwhelming.

November to December was a tricky time of year for

Queensland's drug dealers. The police executed more raids as Schoolies week and Christmas drew nearer; they liked to keep drugs and the associated troublemakers off the street during the holiday period. Consequently, supply could get very low very quickly and I sometimes had to take the risk of dealing with suppliers I didn't really know, let alone trust. The best thing you could do in that situation was carry out the deal in a public place to ensure there was no funny business like a rip-off or even violence. I'd been told the best place to do a public drug deal was at McDonald's. Macca's pretty much has everything you need for a major drug transaction to go down smoothly. There are always plenty of people about, there's lots of parking, everybody is distracted and thinking about food, and there's even a supply of brown paper bags big enough to hide $20,000 cash in.

One day I found myself at a McDonald's on the Gold Coast to meet a new supplier. I went inside, ordered a meal and walked back to my car, where I took the food out of the bag and replaced it with $20,000 in bank notes. I hopped back out and ambled across the car park, where the guy showed me a bag in his car with eight pounds of dope inside. I let him inspect my $20,000 meal deal and hey presto, the business was done before you could say 'Do you want fries with that?'

On another occasion, a major supplier I knew was kind enough to make a home delivery to my place. He gave me the gear and I handed him $14,000.

'You're not going anywhere for a little while are you, Dan?' he asked as he was leaving.

'No, why?' I replied.

'Just wait here for a bit,' he said. 'I'll be back soon to show you something.'

The dude took the fourteen grand to a local motorbike dealership and paid cash for a brand-new bike and then called me on the phone.

'Go and stand outside, man,' he said. 'I'll be there in ten minutes.'

I heard him coming a mile off before he roared into my street on a hulking green machine that sounded like a plane taking off. When he got to my place, he proceeded to do a wheel stand along the full length of the street. I was living in a crazy underworld where money was that liquid. Surely it couldn't last.

—

One thing I had been blessed with in life was an abundance of friends. I genuinely like human beings – a lot. I'm quick to strike up a conversation with new people and I'm careful to nourish existing relationships with phone calls and visits. Still, for some reason, I preferred the company of white people. While I had my tight circle of close friends from Africa who I loved to bits, if I was given the option of hanging out with ten white guys or ten black guys, I'd hang with the white fellas every time. Maybe it goes back to the time I saw that little blond-haired boy on the streets of Juba and wished that my skin could be as milk-white as his.

But after nearly ten years in Australia, many more people

from Africa had entered my orbit in Queensland, as the human wreckage from the war back home sought sanctuary in the West. Hundreds of thousands of South Sudanese refugees had been taken in by the United States, Canada, Australia, New Zealand, the UK and other countries in Western Europe. Part of me may have yearned to be white but I was also proud of my African roots and knew the importance of maintaining our culture after our diaspora.

Although my life was a shambles, I still tried to make sure I respected and honoured the local Sudanese community and stayed connected as much as I could. That's how I came to be sitting in the beautiful Mary Immaculate church in Annerley on a sunny day towards the end of 2004. I'd been invited by a mutual friend to the wedding of a lovely South Sudanese couple. I drove up from the Gold Coast that morning and because it was an important, sacred occasion I didn't want to turn up drunk or stoned. I was still bombed-out on my daily dose of Seroquel but I was otherwise sober and pleased to be part of someone's special day.

After the happy couple had tied the knot and we'd prayed for their happiness, I looked around the church for familiar people to say hello to. As I scanned the crowd to my right, I got the shock of my life when my eyes fell on the face of a man who could not possibly have been there – because he'd died during the war. It was a surreal moment; time slowed and I felt like I was in another dimension for a few seconds. Nah, I thought. It couldn't be! That guy's dead.

I blinked a few times and shook myself a little; I was in a church after all, so maybe God was playing a trick on me.

But when I looked at the man again, there was no ruse and no mistake: it was Anyang, the Red Army's sadistic jailer, monster of my childhood and taker of my tears.

It had been sixteen years since I'd last laid eyes on him, so he was taller as well as older. But everything else was as I remembered from when I was planning to blow his brains out back in 1989. His narrow skull was still perched atop his long neck. His high cheekbones still accentuated the smallness of his mouth and, most of all, his eyes still looked to me like windows into an empty soul.

I locked eyes with him for a moment but I couldn't tell if Anyang recognised me or not, let alone what he might be thinking. I started to tremble but I found myself stuck to the spot. The shock of seeing him again quickly gave way to something else that had been hard-wired deep down inside me for half a lifetime. I had a furious urge to kill him, right then and there in the crowded pews of the church. But we were at a wedding, a sacred gathering where people were laughing, hugging and smiling. I hurried back to my car and sped off.

I'd organised to stay with a friend in Brisbane and on the drive back to his place I fumed as I tried to process what had just happened. I had arrived at a daunting, unexpected crossroads and I struggled to get my emotional bearings. OK, yes, I would get to fulfil my vow to kill Anyang but I knew what that would mean for me – most probably my remaining years would be lived inside the Queensland prison system alongside all the other killers. I had to keep pinching myself to make sure it wasn't just another bad dream about the war – that Anyang was indeed alive and well, and living somewhere in Brisbane. In my mind he was quite literally back from the dead.

Once I arrived at my friend's house I started flashing back to my days in the Red Army camp: Anyang's long, wiry arms raining pitiless blows on me as I writhed facedown in the dirt. The blinding pain. The screams. The menace of hyenas. The little corpses of broken boys. As it all came flooding back, I knew what to do. 'Today, Anyang will die,' I told myself. As I stood up and reached for my car keys I noticed the time: it was late in the afternoon. Sudanese church services always finish at around 2 pm. I'd left it too long; no matter how quickly I got back there, Anyang would have been long gone. Lucky him.

Lucky me.

—

In late 2005 Mary told me she was pregnant. The news somehow penetrated the permanent fog of drugs and alcohol that enveloped my head but I was probably more on the apprehensive side of excited than completely over-joyed. Because I'd lost my dad when I was just a little boy I didn't have any real concept of what was expected of a father – certainly not of fathers in Australia. The echoes of my own dad's role in my life reverberated out of a tribal culture where the raising of children was entirely different from the paternal standpoint.

By any measure, I was totally unprepared for fatherhood. I had no job, I had serious mental health challenges, I had drug and alcohol issues and I relied on crime as a means of providing for myself. Since the arrival of the baby was eight months away, I was able to put the reality of the situation to one side. In the meantime I just kept doing my thing: selling drugs, getting wasted and pondering whether or not I was going to track down Anyang and kill him on the quiet.

Seeing Anyang at the wedding had badly messed with my already messy mind. Although I never told a soul about our silent encounter at the church and I never asked around to see if anyone knew where he lived, I spent a lot of time sitting around stoned, reliving past grievances and pondering exactly how I should end his life. I almost always settled on manual, face-to-face strangulation. Although the flashbacks had subsided I'm told my general mood took a turn for the worse around that time. I could be erratic, volatile and explosive, often to the point of an angry detonation. Over time, though, the desire to crush Anyang's throat started to fade a little and soon enough I was presented with a reason to drop the whole idea to avoid going to prison for the rest of my life.

His name is John, our son, and he was born at the Royal Brisbane and Women's Hospital. I was there to see him come into the world and it was me who chose his name. I was so grateful my boy had been born an Australian. Having had my childhood stolen from me at gunpoint and chased out of my homeland by raiders I thanked God that his first breaths were taken here. No one wanted to harm him and no one would ever terrorise him or run him out of his home. He was born free.

After his arrival, Mary and John continued to spend half of the time in Brisbane at Mary's mum's place and the rest of the time with me at Southport. I think that's when the penny dropped about my drug dealing. Mary implored me to stop.

'Daniel, we've got a child,' she said. 'We need to settle down. I go to work every day and I want you to go to work too. I know you're better than this. You're strong, you're smart, you can get good work somewhere. We can't afford for you to go to jail.'

'Yes, honey, I know, but I'm on medication,' I'd typically reply. 'You know I can't work until I get better.'

'No,' she said. 'You're not going to get any better because you're selling drugs and you're using drugs. We have a child, Daniel, a little boy, and you're running a criminal operation here. Anything could happen. We could get attacked! Anything is possible.'

She was right. One morning I woke up to find all four tyres on my car had been slashed. I may have considered myself Australia's most laidback and popular drug dealer but I was kidding myself. Sometimes I refused to give people credit and sometimes that pissed them off. Drugs can make people do all manner of strange things, as I knew only too well.

By the time my child was born I had been taking anti-psychotic drugs for four years. I had also imbibed huge doses of THC, the psychoactive compound in cannabis that can result in extreme paranoia. Mine had reached a crescendo; my latest neurosis revolved around being a black man with a white partner. Sometimes, if we went on a little family outing to the Australia Fair shopping centre in Southport, I would freak out and refuse to get out of the car.

'What's the matter?' Mary would ask as I locked myself inside the car.

'If I go in there people will look at me and think, "Why is this black guy with a white woman?"' I tried to explain to her. 'Then they'll see we have a little baby together and they're going to hate me. "What is he doing having a baby with a white woman? Who does he think he is?"'

Ever since I came to Australia virtually all of my girl-friends had been white women, something that had never bothered me before. But now I was crippled by the idea and felt like I had to hide away, ashamed of being black and terrified of being judged for the beautiful boy I had helped create.

Poor Mary would have to go and do the shopping by herself and when she'd get back to the car I'd load all the bags in and drive straight home, still convinced people were looking at us, and stewing over what I imagined they were saying about me. I was not well in the head, and *still* I refused to stop selling and smoking the stuff that was making me nuts.

'That's it,' Mary announced one day. 'I'm going to get my own place.'

Rather than freak out, I said I'd help her. I chipped in for the rent of a two-bedroom apartment nearer to her mum in Brisbane.

I hadn't seen it coming and I begged her not to leave

town. 'I'll stop right away,' I promised. But it was too late. Mary was gone. She spent most of her time in Brisbane with our baby and away from me while I continued to kid myself that I was just on the verge of getting my act together.

'I'll finish soon,' I'd promise over the phone. 'I'll stop doing all this bullshit I'm doing, then I'll come and see you.'

By this time I had cut myself off from everyone important in my life. I had even cut myself off from my mum. I would hang up on her whenever she rang and I did the same to John Riedel. Just like Mary, these people cared about me and wanted to help me but I would only get angry and slam the phone down. I didn't care about anyone, least of all myself.

Chaos at the drug house continued unchecked as me and my growing collection of delinquent friends carried on like little boys. My Aussie mate Nick was a regular visitor and one day he arrived with a special gift for me – a python he'd caught during a trip to the farm where he'd grown up.

I was instantly fascinated by this slithering new addition to my already motley household. Even through the haze of drugs and alcohol I lived in, watching that beautifully sinuous body curl and loop took me right back to the innocent joys of my snake-catching days in Awulian when I gleefully followed in the footsteps of my reptile-loving dad.

Although non-venomous, the python had his own tank and sometimes I'd take him out to admire him at closer range. He'd coil so tightly around my arm that my circulation would be cut off, but I was no more afraid of him than I'd been of the many snakes I'd caught back in the grasslands of Twic.

One time when an Aussie mate named Jason was over, we decided to get the python out.

'I wanna see how strong he really is, Jase,' I said. 'Just put him around my neck but hold his head.'

In hindsight, this was taking my interest in reptiles way too far. But by then, my judgement was completely overtaken by the far-reaching grip of past trauma and the toxic chemical assault I subjected myself to night and day.

Jason did as instructed and the python did as expected – it tightened around my throat with alarming speed and strength. That's when Jason let go of the head. In a split second the snake whipped around and bit me on the face but, luckily, it released its grip, dropped onto the carpet and slithered away. I imagine my father would have laughed.

My own life as a dad was stumbling along. Sometimes I'd drive up to Brisbane on the weekends to visit Mary and hold my beautiful little boy. My old Sudanese buddy Michael would run the business while I was away, and if he wasn't around, Nick or Jason would step in and take care of the endless stream of drug addicts who beat a path to my door.

No matter what I promised Mary, I didn't stop. At the time I didn't really know how. My 'lifestyle' had already cost me a proper relationship with my brand-new family and I had lost a large part of my mind along the way, too. If I was going to finally pull free from the tractor beam of self-destruction I would have to lose even more. I needed to take a massive fall before I could start to climb back up again and the way I was heading it was only a matter of time.

16

SHAME

My dreams of working as an actor had all but vanished into a cloud of pot smoke, along with just about every other ambition I had ever held. I'd only had a handful of little roles since I was prescribed Seroquel in 2002. Over the years I kept up the chemical treatment and was monitored by doctors and psychiatrists. All of them deferred to the original diagnosis and stressed how important it was that I keep taking the pills. Almost as soon as I went on Seroquel, however, everything acting-related seemed to stop dead in its tracks.

I did, however, briefly rekindle the belief that I could still make it in the entertainment industry. I can't remember if it was at the suggestion of my old Aussie rapper buddy Alan or not, but one drug-addled day in the mid-2000s I spent $3000 on some high-end home recording equipment. The portable studio not only enabled me to record my own music, it let me burn my own CDs, too! 50 Cent was going to have to watch his back – there was a new MC in town and his name was Trigger Bang, a moniker Alan had dreamed up. I even had an imaginary label: Black Empire Records.

The home studio came pre-programmed with demo hip-hop beats. All I had to do was play one, hit record, start swinging my head and rap into the shiny chrome micro-phone. Simple! But what to rap about? I hadn't really given too much thought to lyrics so I just aped what I'd heard the big stars doing on the radio and in the nightclubs. One of my early efforts went something like this:

Yo, yo, I'm a gangsta – gangsta, killer, hustler and a survivor,

I don't go wrong with the abovementioned activity . . .

Seriously. And then there was this gem:

Fuck the police, Black Empire Records: police's hell and the graveyard . . .

It really wasn't me. I had never pretended to be a homie, a gangsta or even remotely hip-hop. People could say what they wanted about me but one thing they'd all agree on was that I was authentic.

I normally wasn't even interested in songs about 'mutha-fuckas cappin' niggaz, bitches and snitches'. I was a Slim Dusty fan, for God's sake! My short-lived home-recording career showed just how deluded I'd become – how unshack-led from reality. I truly believed I was on the verge of becoming a major rap artist. Yeah, man, I thought. I'll just buy a home studio and make it happen. I soon put the thing away and went back to listening to the music I liked. Music by Bob Dylan. Music that made me think. Music that made me realise I was just blowin' in the wind.

By 2008 I was not only mentally feeble, I was underweight, physically drawn and very weak. My mood could turn in a split second and I had grown even more paranoid. I was still driving up the M1 to visit my son regularly, and sometimes Mary and John would come and stay with me in Southport.

This difficult arrangement was getting more and more emotionally fraught. The main point of contention? Mary's concern about my ability to look after my son properly. At the time I just couldn't understand her reservations, and my heart broke to contemplate the possibility I'd lose from my life yet another soul I loved with all my being, the way family and friends had been torn from me during those war years.

One day I turned things very ugly. I arrived at Mary's apartment in Brisbane, self-medicated to the eyeballs on my usual cocktail of drugs and alcohol, only to be told she didn't want me to spend time alone with my son anymore.

'And I don't want him going to that house again,' she said, gesturing south towards my place down the coast. 'Just look at you! I don't want him to be with you. I'm frightened for him!'

I had been trying to shove reality – with all its despair and disappointment – out of my consciousness with substances for the best part of six years. Sadly, I was so far gone I still couldn't grasp what the problem was, even though it should have been as clear as day.

'Why, Mary? Why, why, why? Please, let's work something out!'

We argued bitterly but she stuck to her guns.

'I don't want him to be with you!' she shouted. 'He's a little boy! He doesn't belong in a drug house!'

Until the day I die I will never stop being ashamed about what I did next: I violently threw Mary to the ground and started hitting her. By that stage of my life I had chalked up some truly terrible acts that I have regretted ever since. But the very worst of these is striking a woman. Striking Mary, the girl of my dreams and the mother of my beloved boy.

The police were called and, since I had breached my parole again, I was sent back to prison to receive the punishment I richly deserved.

That day in April 2008 marked the very last time I ever visited my son at his mother's home. It heralded the end of whatever relationship I had with Mary and it was also the last day I ever smoked weed. That's what it took to get me to stop – a jail term following the assault occasioning actual bodily harm to a person I loved most in the world. I knew I would never get her back – after what I did I didn't deserve her – but if I didn't start trying to fix myself now I likely never would, and that would mean I'd lose my son, too.

There was a time on the outside where I couldn't go one hour without smoking weed, but in jail I had to stop immediately. I'd done that before, during my first stint in jail, and it hadn't worried me in the slightest. In the years since, though, I had drastically upped my intake and it had clearly messed with my brain chemistry. People say withdraw-ing from heroin is like going to hell and back but I found withdrawing from years of chronic marijuana intake had its side effects, too. I developed a bad case of the shakes that seemed like it might never stop. I was still taking my daily dose of Seroquel, which meant I'd at least get to sleep at night. Had I not taken it, I might have suffered the nerve-jangling tremors 24/7.

It was one thing to give up pot, though, and another to quit the lifestyle I'd followed for years selling drugs. The temptation was just too great after I found there was a black market for pills in a prison, just as there had been for bullets during the war. Any kind of mind-numbing or sedative medication is valuable in jail and extremely hard for the average inmate to get. Since I was a diagnosed schizophrenic I had no trouble. In fact, I told the prison medical staff I couldn't sleep and they upped my dose from two three-hundred-milligram tablets a day to four per day. The truth was, I only needed two in order to sleep properly: one in the morning and one at night. But now I was getting a double dose I had to find a way of keeping the extra tablets to sell.

As a boy in the village I used to regurgitate my food. Meals were often meagre and once you'd eaten your portion there was no seconds and no popping out to the shops to get a snack. So, to at least give myself the illusion I was eating more, I would draw the food back up into my mouth and chew on it some more and swallow it again, just like a cow. I perfected the technique in prison with Seroquel.

Inmates who were on medication had to line up in the morning and evening at the nurses' station to receive our pills under strict supervision. A prison guard would watch me put the pill in my mouth and wash it down with water. Then I had to open my mouth wide so the officer could take a good look inside to make sure it had gone down the hatch.

I would swallow the first tablet completely but when I put the second one in my mouth I let the water wash past it, then I'd let the pill drop into the back of my throat before opening my mouth for inspection. The guard would see it was empty but he had no idea I was able to regurgitate the thing thirty seconds later ready for sale to the highest bidder. By pulling my ruse I was able to make money to spend at the prison canteen.

The tremors from marijuana withdrawal had stopped by the time I was released four months later, but it wasn't the only change I noticed. Without the weed, everything seemed a little clearer and less confusing, as if a veil had been lifted from my eyes. That's not to say I felt anywhere near normal. I continued to drink excessively, with the added excuse that I needed a little help to get to sleep now that cannabis was out of my system. Although I wasn't quite as befuddled by drugs, I was still mentally unwell. I had also fallen into a deep depression fuelled by crushing shame over what I had done and the fact I was not allowed to see my boy.

I spent a lot of time on the couch thinking about suicide again. For some strange reason, I felt as though I deserved to die on the roads of Queensland. Perhaps it was related to my track record for cheating death behind the wheel. After mulling it over for weeks, I figured a good way to go would be to open up the passenger door of a car travelling at a hundred and twenty kilometres per hour and just dive out onto the highway.

I never followed through with it. Instead, I would soon almost kill myself and others completely by accident.

Upon my release from jail I was paroled with a $10,000 surety to be paid by my old high school teacher and mentor John Riedel should I run afoul of the law. While I'd been locked up in Arthur Gorrie Correctional Centre I also lost the tenancy of my Gold Coast townhouse and, along with it, the drug-dealing. I was happy to let the enterprise wither and die. I was done with drugs, which pretty much meant I was done with the Gold Coast, too, since just about everything I had ever done during my years living there was related to the purchase, sale and ingestion of mass quantities of dope.

The conditions of my parole required me to attend drug and alcohol treatment, and an anger management program. I also had to reside at John Riedel's house in Toowoomba, with a 7 pm curfew and I was required to 'sign in' at Toowoomba police station by 3 pm every afternoon. If I didn't, a warrant would be issued for my arrest and I'd be sent back to jail. Despite the restrictions, I was eager to move to Brisbane and have the parole transferred there so I could at least be closer to my son.

All of the lazy, tainted money I'd made selling drugs

was long gone and where I once drove a $36,000 sports car I now got around in a busted-up green Ford Falcon I'd bought for $3000. I started making quick daytrips down the freeway to Brisbane in order to fill out applications for rental properties in the city before driving back to Toowoomba and signing in at the police station in the afternoon.

On one such run to the city I was joined by some friends. We started drinking before we even breached the outskirts of Toowoomba. I spent the morning visiting real estate agents and looking at units to lease in Brisbane before I headed over to my old friend Michael's place. That's where the force of habit took over and I set myself on a path that was always going to end badly. With Michael and my two friends Kyle and Fred, I sat around drinking the afternoon away. At about 1 pm I informed them I needed to be back in Toowoomba to sign in by 3 pm otherwise I'd be in the shit. But I was in no state to decide how to legally and safely make that happen. Once again, old habits held sway and I reached for my car keys.

'OK, man, let's do it!' said Michael, rising unsteadily to his feet. 'We're coming with you!'

Once a plan of action was decided, the four of us threw ourselves into the mission as enthusiastically as we could, considering the condition we were in. After piling sloppily into the Ford, we stopped at a bottle-o around the corner to buy more booze before turning up the stereo and heading west for the hills. Before too long, however, Fred told me to drop him at Ipswich train station along the way. He had read the danger signs. 'Hey, Dan, I'm gunna get a train back to Brisbane instead,' he said. Smart move.

It was a beautiful, warm afternoon in south-east Queensland and as we cruised west along the Warrego Highway we got steadily more drunk on cans of Jim Beam. Although the Ford was no match for the mighty Supra, I still managed to push it up to a hundred and thirty kilometres per hour, well over the speed limit even with three big guys onboard.

About halfway to Toowoomba I came up fast behind a slow-moving car travelling in the left lane. As I yanked the wheel to the right to overtake it, I clipped the other car's rear bumper. It didn't affect the trajectory of that vehicle but the collision sent the Ford wildly out of control. The big green box jerked and swerved left off the highway. A millisecond later we careened through bushland at well over a hundred kilometres per hour, though it felt like we were crashing in slow motion. I knew that if I touched the brakes there was a chance the car would flip and roll over, so I just held onto the steering wheel for dear life, put my head down and hoped for the best.

The runaway Ford cut a neat path through thick bushes and smaller trees that shattered the windscreen and crumpled the bonnet. Finally we came to a jarring halt less than a metre from a huge gum tree that would have likely killed us had we hit it as soon as we left the road.

'Is everybody all right?' I called out as we all checked ourselves for signs of injury. Thankfully, the boys weren't even scratched.

I blurrily assessed the predicament I'd put myself in. Even through my haze, I knew if I was arrested and charged with drink-driving I would be in breach of my parole and sent straight back to prison. I would be separated from my son for a very, very long time. In my head at that moment, right or wrong didn't come into it. I just felt like I couldn't risk that happening – at any cost.

A number of people had witnessed the crash, including the driver whose car I had clipped. They would no doubt tell the police all about the tall black man wearing a white polo shirt who'd been at the wheel. The first thing I did when we pulled ourselves clear of the wrecked Ford was whip that shirt off.

'Look, boys, I'm going to run,' I told the others. 'I don't want to go back to jail. If the police come and ask you who the driver was, just tell them it was some Jamaican guy named James who you met at a club. But the car belongs to your friend Daniel. OK?'

'OK.' The guys nodded.

And with that, I was off. I'd crashed in a semi-rural part of the Lockyer Valley that was scattered with stands of gum trees, and with a few farmhouses dotted here and there. I ran about two kilometres over the low hills, crossed a creek or two, jumped a few fences and ditched my white shirt along the way.

After I clambered over one particularly high fence I was alarmed to find I had lowered myself into a paddock that was home to an angry-looking bull. As soon as we locked eyes he charged at me.

I ran for my life and managed to throw myself over

another fence, which put me in the backyard of a two-storey farmhouse where an elderly couple sat on the balcony watching me with quizzical expressions on their faces. I waved at them meekly and the old guy came down to talk to me.

'What happened to you, mate?' he said with a concerned look.

'Oh, I was just attacked in the local pub!' I lied, panting for breath.

The silver-haired guy ushered me inside the house, gave me a shirt to wear and handed me a glass of water. 'So, tell me again,' he said, 'exactly what happened?'

'Me and my two friends were driving from Brisbane and going to Toowoomba,' I began. 'We just had a quick stop at the pub down the highway for a few drinks when we were attacked by a group of bikies. They just started bashing us for no reason!'

The old guy frowned sympathetically. 'Oh, that's terrible.'

'Yeah,' I agreed. 'I don't know why – I think they probably don't like black people.'

'Some people are awful,' he said, gently shaking his head.

As we chatted away about the make-believe brawl, I kept fretting about my 3 pm appointment with the Toowoomba police. If I failed to turn up on time, there was a good chance I'd be sent back to jail anyway, regardless of whether I ended up getting caught for the drunken freeway crash.

'Listen,' I said to the old couple, 'I have about $40 and I really need to be back in Toowoomba urgently for a three o'clock appointment. I don't suppose you could drive me there if I gave you some money for petrol?'

They said they'd be only too happy. I had jumped into the backyard of the nicest couple in Queensland. About twenty minutes later I was sitting in the back seat of their luxury four-wheel drive when I received a text message from Kyle.

Cops & ambos here. Cops looking for driver & stopping cars on hwy 2 c if driver was picked up.

I figured the police wouldn't pull us over because the nice couple appeared too old and sensible to pick up a black man running along the highway. Still, I put my head down every time I saw a car approaching or passing us.

We arrived in Toowoomba about 2.45 pm and I asked the couple to drop me off just down the street from the police station. I gave them the petrol money and thanked them profusely, and as they drove off I bolted down the street. When I neared the police station I slowed to a walk and then casually mooched inside as though I had just ambled in from watching TV next door. The officers hadn't the faintest idea I had just caused a high-speed car crash and been chased by a snorting bull.

I signed the book and sauntered back outside to call Kyle.

'Heya, D,' he said. 'We were taken back to Ipswich Hospital for a check-up but we're all good.'

'Oh that's great, man. I'm glad you're OK,' I said. 'What did the cops say about the driver?'

'We told them it was a Jamaican guy named James who

we met at a nightclub in Brisbane the night before,' Kyle
parroted. 'But there was a woman who stopped right after
the crash because she was a nurse. She started saying the
driver didn't look Jamaican at all – she said he was a black
African instead. But we all said, "Nah, he was a Jamaican
dude, James. We only met him last night."'

Even I had to admit it was an unlikely story, and over the
next few days I kept expecting the cops to knock on John
Riedel's door and arrest me, but it never happened. I'm not
at all proud of the mayhem I caused or my deception afterwards, but back then it felt worth it to save any shred of
relationship with my son that I possibly could.

Also, kicking my drug habit had by no means given me
mental clarity. I had only managed it by upping my alcohol
intake. I was also downing the Seroquel and I sometimes
wondered whether I was ever going to stop being a schizophrenic. The continued drink-driving, the highway crash
and my disregard for my own and other people's safety was
of great concern. Clearly I had a lot of mental and emotional problems, not least with substance abuse, but no one
seemed to think my behaviour related to the dark tangle
of trauma caused by my experiences as a child soldier.
Not even me.

In a few short years I had gone from someone who rarely
drank to someone who was rarely not drunk. I had become
one of those people who never turned down an opportunity to consume alcohol. I would drink alone, with friends,
with strangers, at parties, in parks, at home, in the car, in
nightclubs, at night, in the morning . . . I didn't care, so

long as I was hosing my problems down with alcohol and trying to drown my inner demons.

I was in the midst of a run-of-the-mill drinking session at a Sudanese friend's house in Brisbane when I was again presented with the opportunity I used to dream about as a tortured Red Army trainee.

I saw Anyang again. This time I was full of enough Dutch courage that I walked right up and confronted him.

'Do you remember me?' I asked him flatly.

'Yes, Ayik Chut,' he replied.

'Do you remember what you did to me during the training?' I pressed.

'Yes, of course I do,' he said softly.

'Anyang, you are a lucky man,' I said. 'Australia has saved your life. I wanted to kill you so bad when we were in Africa but I had no power then.'

He just stared at the floor.

'I didn't want to use a gun, Anyang,' I continued. 'I wanted to kill you with my bare hands, to torture you slowly until you died.'

'I am really sorry for everything I have done to you,' he said, still looking downwards.

'Nah, it's OK, man,' I assured him. 'It's this beautiful country that saved you. It saved me, too, many times over and that's why I owe it to myself and to Australia not to kill you. So you go now, Anyang – go and live your life and be happy.'

When I woke up hung over the next day I thought back to what I'd said to Anyang. Did I really mean it?

I puzzled to myself. Did *he* really mean it? Was he really sorry? I accepted that I would likely never know.

—

For nearly eight years I started most days by putting three hundred milligrams of Seroquel into my mouth and washing it down with a glass of water. That was just the way schizo-phrenia was treated, the doctors kept telling me. Every time I went to see my GP or my psychiatrist they were anxious to know that I was dosing myself in the way that had been prescribed.

'Have you been taking your drugs, Mr Chut?' they'd ask.

'Yes, sir,' I'd reply.

'You know you have to keep taking them if you want to get better.'

'Oh yes, of course.'

Only I wasn't getting any better. I didn't even know what having schizophrenia was supposed to feel like but I sure knew what Seroquel dependence felt like: completely numb. Immediately after I swallowed my morning dose, I'd collapse onto the couch in front of the TV. I could be stranded in front of daytime television for hours because I could barely move or even reach the remote control twenty centimetres away.

I would tell the doctors, 'It's not working!' Occasionally they would listen and put me on a course of some other elephant tranquiliser for a month or two, but I always ended up back on the dreaded Seroquel.

By 2010, long after the marijuana haze had lifted, I felt an overwhelming compulsion to be the best man I could be for the sake of my little boy. Even though I was not permitted to make contact with his mother, by now I had limited access to our son under strict supervision and I wanted those cherished times to be as crystal clear, happy, honest and as loving as they possibly could be. Seroquel didn't fit into that picture.

Medicos had meddled with my brain chemistry for years and I had nothing to show for it. In fact, my troubles could be traced back to the initial diagnosis and the first script for Seroquel in 2002. Everything bad in my life happened after that: the illicit drugs, the alcohol abuse, the drink-driving, the fights, prison, the drug dealing, the outbursts, the violence at home, the suicidal thoughts and my loss of all ambition.

I was now renting a modest apartment in the Brisbane suburb of Nundah and I badly wanted to get my life together. I peered into the mirror one morning to see a haunted-looking man with sunken cheeks and dead eyes staring back at me. Instead of swallowing my medication I flushed the tablets down the toilet. Screw the doctors, I thought to myself. I'm doing this cold turkey.

I knew it was going to be a dark, painful journey but I didn't expect withdrawal to last for years. I felt OK for the first few days because little molecules of Seroquel were still floating around in my body, but after a week it was as if my blood had dried out inside my veins. I felt brittle, paper-thin, extremely agitated and unable to sleep a wink.

After a month of no sleep whatsoever I felt like death might be a better option. I would lie on my couch or in bed feeling that my body was made out of wet sand. Half of my brain screamed furiously for that little pill and some water to wash it down. No! I don't need it! the other half of my mind would stonewall. I don't want it. I'm going to be free.

I cried for hours every day, praying to God to just let me have one hour of sleep. My poor body was as good as dead but my brain was on high alert, plotting and scheming for a chemical interlude. But I held firm and I finally started to drift off for an hour here and there. Then, sometimes, I would fall asleep and not wake up for two to three hours at a time.

It was still a nightmarish existence and, desperate for at least someone to talk to about it, I went to my GP.

'I stopped taking the Seroquel,' I told her bluntly.

'Well, you definitely should not have done that,' she replied. 'You won't be better off without it and you'll likely have episodes of—'

'No, enough!' I told her. 'I am not better! The drugs only hurt me. They have done nothing but bring me pain. My life has only gotten worse and worse since I started taking them. I am done with them. No more!'

All the GP could do was listen and when I had finished, she looked me in the eye and said, 'Would you at least go and have an assessment from a psychiatrist?'

A month or so later I met with a new psychiatrist, who listened very carefully to my story. He seemed sympathetic and said he would have to examine my full mental health history before we could go any further. 'In the meantime,' he added, 'why don't you do what the GP says and resume taking your medication?'

'That's not going to happen,' I replied. 'It's killing me.'

On my second appointment, he sat me down with a folder crammed full of my so-called mental problems. It was apparent to him, having spoken to me and studied my records, that the initial diagnosis of schizophrenia in 2002 had been completely wrong. Perhaps the original psychiatrist had been influenced by the way I communicated, given my limited grasp of English. Or maybe he had taken my admission of smoking a bit of pot into consideration and made more of it than was necessary. Perhaps it was a combination of factors but whatever it was, the new psychiatrist arrived at a different conclusion.

The only mental health diagnosis is post-traumatic stress disorder in partial remission, he wrote. *There is a past diagnosis of cannabis-induced psychosis. Ayik does not have schizophrenia and never had schizophrenia.*

Although I felt relieved and vindicated, I was also wary of being told I suffered from PTSD. What if it was another misdiagnosis? I had trusted doctors before and they had put me on the wrong drug, and encouraged me to take it for eight years! Even though I was in 'partial remission' from PTSD (which apparently meant I was mostly OK), the psychiatrist told me he could treat any symptoms that might come up from time to time with some kind of medication.

'No way,' I said flatly. 'I'm never taking drugs again.

They ruined my life for eight years and I'm not going back there.'

Today I remain one hundred per cent drug free – I won't even take Panadol. Give me a simple headache any day.

Looking back, the signs that I had suffered badly from PTSD were clear. The first symptoms appeared when I was in high school in the form of recurring nightmares. Those were followed by the kitchen bench hallucinations about stabbing my young relatives, not to mention my wildly explosive emotional state. It didn't help that I kept all of it to myself, but that was just the African way. And it certainly didn't help that I self-medicated with marijuana and alcohol.

Although I was relieved not be a 'schizophrenic' any-more, I still had to endure the horrors of the sleepless Seroquel withdrawal.

Not long after I quit the pills I landed the first legitimate job I'd had since I'd worked as a sales rep for Foxtel eight years earlier. I joined Brisbane City Council as a green-keeper at St Lucia Golf Links and attained a certificate in horticulture along the way.

The job helped me steady the ship when it came to with-drawal; I'd put in a hard, physical day's work and then catch a train home, where I'd pass out for a few hours and wake around midnight only to lie in bed until 4 am when I'd start to get ready to catch a 5 am train back to work.

All those dark, lonely hours gave me plenty of time for reflection. I would think about where I had been, the mistakes I had made and the direction in which I was heading. Although I would think back to my past incarnations as a tribal boy and a Red Army soldier, it had been many years since I had nightmares about death, blood and war. Sometimes I would lie awake at 3 am and wonder if Anyang was awake in another part of the city, tormented by the things he had seen and done.

Although I had granted Anyang my half-hearted, drunken forgiveness I felt we had unfinished business. I still yearned to hear him confess in full to all of his sins and to apologise for everything he had done, not only to me but all the other kids he had tortured.

For years I had wondered whether any boys had died under Anyang's rule as the Red Army's punisher-in-chief. I'd never forgotten the poor little guy who lost his arms but I couldn't help thinking that maybe worse things happened in the Red Army prison. I'd roll over and the garish green numbers on the digital clock would show 4.10 am – time to rise and shine and get ready for work.

Some nights I'd spend hours spooling back through my lost years when I was a drug user and dope dealer, and wonder how I ever got so far off track. My god, how could I have been violent towards Mary? I'd been so grateful for the opportunities Australia had given; when I first arrived I was one hundred per cent focused on making the most of every day. I had studied hard and worked hard trying to make a good life for myself. I wanted Australia to be proud that it had given me and my loved ones sanctuary and kindness. Instead, everything turned to shit extraordinarily quickly.

It's not like I didn't have good influences or people who tried to help pull me out of the downwards spiral. Had I listened to them, things would have been different. We would have been a family and I would have worked hard to provide for Mary and my son, like millions of other dads. Maybe we'd have had another child. Ironically, it was Mary's complete withdrawal from my life that finally got through to me and caused me to change – however horrible the process had been and however appallingly I had acted.

Three years after I tipped the Seroquel down the toilet I finally started sleeping relatively normally. While my routines and patterns were still fairly random, I had at least survived the terrible phase during which I subsisted on one to three hours a day. I started to feel more like me and less like a ghost. Heartened by the dawning feeling of normality, I decided it would be a good idea to stop drinking, too.

Alcohol and I had never been a good mix. Most of the bad decisions I had ever made – from threatening people with an anti-tank grenade to striking the love of my life and mother of my child – were made when I was drunk. My abysmal driving record, which included multiple DUI charges, could be attributed to booze. So could many other obnoxious offences I had been charged with over the years. My early flirtations with sobriety came about because of my son – I never wanted to be drunk when I had access visits with him and I noticed how good my clear head made me feel about myself. Midway through 2013 I had my last ever taste of alcohol.

Although going to jail after the domestic violence charge

had been the impetus for turning my life around, it took me a long time to pull myself together and I did it in stages. I started by quitting marijuana in 2008, followed by getting off Seroquel cold turkey in 2010 and, finally, giving up alcohol in 2013. It goes to show how deep a hole I had dug myself into that it took me five years to drag myself back out.

Tellingly, my history with medication and substance abuse is clearly reflected in my criminal record. The first of my twenty-six court appearances occurred in December 2002 just after I was prescribed Seroquel, and the last was in May 2013 just before I stopped drinking. I often wonder about the man I would have otherwise been. Now that I was back in the land of the living, however, the big question was 'What am I going to do with my life now?'

17

LOOK ME IN THE EYE

My new career as a council greenkeeper came to a sudden, painful end early one morning after an overnight storm had toppled a tree at St Lucia Golf Links. As my work partner cut the branches off the tree with a chainsaw, I was tasked with yanking them clear. When I tugged hard on one of the boughs, I slipped and fell backwards awkwardly, badly fracturing my left wrist and damaging the ligaments as I hit the ground.

Unable to use my hand properly, I spent eighteen months on WorkCover compensation payments and had to undergo two rounds of surgery trying to fix my mangled wrist. To alleviate the boredom of sitting at home, and to feel like I was contributing to society, I volunteered at the Brisbane Homelessness Services Centre. I worked on reception and did some data entry for them too. It was fulfilling and I was glad to help people less fortunate than myself in some small way but I preferred the physical side of things and was anxious to get back to work as a greenkeeper.

During the first operation, though, the ligament was removed from my wrist and replaced with a piece of muscle harvested from my forearm. I was told it would never be the same again and my days of manual labour were over. I was devastated.

Suddenly at another crossroads, I had to figure out what I was going to do with myself. After thinking on it for a while I realised the one thing that had remained a consistent passion was the idea of working in the movie business – a dream that had its roots in an Ethiopian tree from where I first saw Arnold Schwarzenegger in *Commando*. My acting had almost taken flight with the encouragement of my first girlfriend Kristy, but then ten years of my life went missing in the fog of drugs and booze.

Being drug- and alcohol-free was a bit like waking up from a terrible dream. It was a slow but sweet process – almost the reverse of getting wasted. Each day as I adjusted to my new clarity, the ebb and flow of life became easier to handle. I still had my problems but now I could see them more plainly and address them properly. I also started to dream a little and set some goals.

I may have been a mixed-up individual but I was never so befuddled that I thought I could make it as a lead actor. I had, however, already shown I was useful in local productions as an extra. I figured acting was something anyone could do – even if they were injured, even if they'd gotten a bit older and even if they suffered from PTSD or made mistakes. By now my English was pretty good, too, so I reconnected with my old agent and told him I wanted to get back to work.

The change in my fortune was huge. Pretty soon I was cast as an extra in the blockbuster film *San Andreas* starring Dwayne 'The Rock' Johnson. Although the film is about a catastrophic earthquake that strikes California, the whole thing was shot on my home turf in Brisbane, the Gold Coast and the Lockyer Valley. Dwayne Johnson plays a helicopter pilot who has to somehow save his family from disaster, while I play a much lesser-known role: a man dressed in a suit standing inside an office.

Other Hollywood films followed. I appeared as an extra in *Aquaman* with Jason Momoa and Amber Heard, *Dora and the Lost City of Gold* starring Eva Longoria and Benicio del Toro, and I even auditioned for a speaking role in *Thor: Ragnarok* alongside Aussie superstars Chris Hemsworth and Cate Blanchett. Although I didn't get the part, the casting director kept me on as an extra because of how I looked.

I was taken for costume fittings and a few weeks later I received my call sheet, listing details of the shooting dates and times I was required. The movie was being filmed at the Village Roadshow Studios on the Gold Coast and sometimes they wanted cast and crew there at 3 am. I'd have to get up for work at 2 am, drive down the M1, sign in, go to the extras' waiting room, have a costume fitting and get my hair and make-up done, eat some breakfast and then line up to be checked over before I could go on set.

I played five different characters in *Thor: Ragnarok*, which required five different costume fittings for just one humble extra. In three of the scenes my face was covered by a mask – including a lion's head – but in the other two my face was fully visible onscreen to audiences around the world.

In one scene I was among a group of Asgard fighters who had to beat up Chris Hemsworth, the Hollywood star playing Thor, after he was caught in a net. He fell to the ground, his head landing right at my feet, and I clubbed him with the butt of my rifle. I couldn't help feeling a bit sorry for him. He was Chris Hemsworth, after all. Not Thor! I didn't really want to bash his head in at work so it was a fine line between acting realistically and hurting the guy. After a few takes of the scene, however, Chris stood up and said, 'You guys are not hitting me hard enough!'

OK then, I thought. I'll give you some hits to remember.

During the next take I laid into Chris properly, raining blow after blow around his shoulders. When the director yelled, 'Cut!' Chris got to his feet, patted me on the back and said, 'That was a good one.'

In my head I was thinking, Yeah, you don't muck around with a child soldier! I was trained to beat enemies to death with the butt of a gun if I ever ran out of bullets.

I got an enormous thrill working on film sets, seeing how the magic is conjured behind the scenes and having the opportunity to work alongside some of the most famous actors in the world: people like Jeff Goldblum, Idris Elba and Sir Anthony Hopkins. Considering the smouldering ruins of my earlier life, I sometimes had to pinch myself.

The art often imitated my life, too, which could be kind of strange. In the film *Australia Day*, featuring Bryan Brown, I appeared in a class full of multicultural students, and in the TV series *Wanted*, with Rebecca Gibney, I played an inmate who is seen kissing his girlfriend when she visits him in jail. My teenage self would have gagged at the thought.

In the movie *Don't Tell* I was cast as a nicely dressed man who walks into a courthouse to face the music for a crime he committed. The film starred the legendary Aussie actor Jack Thompson. I'd first heard of him not long after we arrived in Australia. Getting to appear in the same film as Jack was a great honour because I considered him a cultural icon from his role as Clancy of the Overflow in *The Man from Snowy River*. I watched him closely as he acted in *Don't Tell*, hoping to pick up some of his skills.

When I was diagnosed with PTSD, I qualified for a disability pension. I tried to get work, and since I earned very little from acting I paid the rent by working as an Uber and taxi driver in between gigs. The rest of the time I focused hard on being the best possible father to my son, although I still wasn't seeing him as much as I wanted to.

I finally got my first speaking role in 2017 after I auditioned for a part in the Australian TV series *Safe Harbour*, starring Jacqueline McKenzie and Hazem Shammas. The show was set in Brisbane and told the story of a group of friends whose sailing trip to Indonesia is interrupted when they come across a boat overloaded with asylum seekers. In yet another case of art imitating life, I played one of the desperate refugees. I even had a scene with Hazem Shammas, who went on to win the Logie award for Most Outstanding Supporting Actor, which made me feel pretty good.

To boost my chances of getting more roles I started doing relevant courses in fields like stunt training. I also had a lot of support from a filmmaker friend named Temucin Mustafa. He taught me a lot about how to deliver lines and he encouraged me to study more.

Following Temucin's advice, I spent two years gaining an advanced diploma of screen and stage acting from the Australian Performing Arts Conservatory in Brisbane. One day, another friend in the entertainment industry suggested I do some weapons training to help me play a gangster or in a military role.

'Dude, I'm an ex-child soldier,' I scoffed. 'I know how to use guns! I was doing it since I was nine years old.'

'Well, the thing is, it's not like what you did in the war using live ammunition,' he said. 'That's totally different from training for the movies. They use props and blank rounds, and they're after a certain look.'

I figured I didn't have anything to lose so I found an armourer who specialised in weapons instruction for film and TV. When I turned up at the training complex the following Saturday morning, I was amazed when he pulled an AK-47 out of a box.

'Oh, man!' I exclaimed. 'Is that thing a fake?'

'Nah, mate,' the armourer responded. 'It's a real AK-47.'

'That's my gun!' I told him excitedly. 'I used that all my life when I was in Africa and I never, ever thought I would see one again – definitely not here in Australia.'

He started off by showing me how to handle smaller guns and I easily fired a pistol loaded with blank rounds, but when we moved on to the AK-47 I was transported straight from laid-back Queensland to a fractured Sudan. I hadn't been sure how I would feel holding the gun again but when the armourer loaded it with blanks and handed it to me, all I wanted to do was fire it.

He filmed me as I let rip with the Kalashnikov on the gun range created on an industrial lot, and a few days later when I reviewed the video at home, I noticed how different it looked and felt from when I carried one in Africa. Something just didn't seem to fit. For one thing, the gun had felt much lighter at the armourer's range and I seemed to have far more control over the weapon. Then it dawned on me in a rush of emotions: the gun may have been exactly the same but I had changed – a lot. I wasn't a skinny, malnourished little boy anymore; I didn't tremble with fear when I pulled the trigger and the gun didn't try to throw me backwards.

I steadily fell more and more in love with acting. In an odd way, it gave me a sense of freedom and escape from some of the hardships of my past and the humdrum of the daily grind. Whether I was cast as an Asgard warrior, an office worker or a bank robber I got to step into the make-believe shoes of some other life for a little while and do things I'd never get to do in reality. So it came as a great surprise when the most liberating role of my life simply called for me to appear as myself.

Always on the lookout for new roles, in early 2017 I logged on to a website called Star Now, which matches producers and casting directors with actors and performers. That's when I saw an SBS TV casting call looking for people to take part in a new program called *Look Me in the Eye*. The premise of the show was to take two people who had been estranged for whatever reason, sit them in a room and have them look into each other's eyes for five minutes. After that, the participants are asked if they'd like to try to reconnect and reconcile by talking through their grievances.

'Boy,' I said to myself, 'do I have a story for you guys at SBS.'

I sent a long note to the producers explaining that I was a former child soldier from South Sudan who had unexpectedly run into a person who used to torture me during the war. I explained how I'd thought Anyang was dead until I saw him during a church service years later. *For a long time I wanted to take my revenge and kill him*, I explained. *But it's been hanging over me for so long now I just want to see him again, to truly forgive him and move on with my life*. The pitch not only got their attention, but it became the lead story in the first episode.

Although Mary Immaculate Church in Annerley was a popular place of worship among Brisbane's Sudanese community, I had never returned for fear of coming face to face with Anyang again. In spite of the fact that twice before I'd resisted my temptation to exact a brutal revenge, I still worried that the lion inside me might one day rise up and tear him apart. So it was a particularly intense day when an SBS crew took me back to the church to re-enact the fateful day. Thankfully it was a weekday, so no congregation was there but I felt very emotional sitting in the same pews where I'd gotten the shock of my life all those years before.

I'd made some inquiries within Brisbane's South Sudanese circles and managed to find a phone number for Anyang, which I passed on to SBS. The day before filming, I was flown from Brisbane to Sydney – the first time I'd been on a plane since I touched down in Australia twenty-one years earlier. There were no ham sandwiches on offer this time.

I was driven to a warehouse in inner-city Sydney, where SBS had created a set to film the episodes of *Look Me in the Eye*. I was greeted outside the warehouse by the show's host, the respected TV journalist Ray Martin.

Ray was inquisitive and sensitive as he interviewed me about my time as a child soldier, the treatment I had received at the hands of Anyang and how I wanted to be the best man possible so my son could have a father to be proud of.

The people at SBS are very smart and know how to capture true reactions and emotions. For instance, the very first time I met Ray Martin was when they filmed me actually walking up to meet him outside the warehouse. At that stage I had no idea whether Anyang was even going to turn up. If he didn't, I asked Ray to tell him that I forgave him anyway.

'What if you do get to look him in the eye?' Ray asked.

'I just want to see and feel that he is sorry,' I said. 'Does he have remorse for what he's done? Because what he did to me has affected my life since I was a kid. I just want it to come to an end and the time is today.'

Then Ray left me to wait for my time on camera. As I sat fretting, still unaware that Anyang was even in town, in another room Ray was on set opposite my nemesis and commencing the interview. 'Let's go back to Sudan,' Ray said to Anyang. 'When were you taken as a boy soldier?'

'I remember this was in 1983,' Anyang began. 'This was on May the sixteenth. Yes, I remember the day because that was the first day I heard the sound of a gun.'

Anyang explained that his parents were killed on that day, along with his brother and sister. He didn't say who killed his family, only that he somehow survived and made it to the relative safety of Ethiopia. 'When we arrived in Ethiopia I got no person to stay with and there was a military camp,' Anyang revealed. 'So I got no choice . . . I have to go to the camp.'

Ray steered the conversation to Anyang's experiences during the war, after he'd served as the prison warden in the Red Army. 'Did you see a lot of killing?' he asked Anyang gently.

'Yes,' Anyang replied.

'Hundreds?' Ray pressed.

'I think more than that because I been in war zone for almost eleven years,' Anyang said.

When he told Ray he had likely seen thousands of

people slaughtered during the war, the veteran journalist dug deeper.

'Anyang,' he said, 'what was the worst day when you think back on those eleven years you were a soldier?'

Anyang took a deep breath as he called the memory to mind. 'We were given an order to attack the enemies,' he said. 'So when we start firing, enemies come from this direction and this direction in front of us. So we [numbered] two thousand six hundred. The number [of boy soldiers] that returned back was one thousand and fourteen.'

'So you lost over one thousand boys?' Ray asked.

'Yeah, including myself,' Anyang added. 'I was shot twice, too.'

The conversation then moved back to the period leading up to Anyang's deployment, when he was in charge of punishing wayward child soldiers like me in the Red Army camp.

'When did you become the camp guard of these boys?' Ray asked.

'This was in 1988,' Anyang stated, 'because I was given a promotion. I was told, "Now you have to go and train the Red Army so they can become good soldiers."'

Anyang said he was only sixteen when he was assigned to 'train' the rest of us, including boys aged as young as ten.

'But you're the boss?' Ray said.

'I'm the boss,' Anyang agreed, 'but I've got other boss ahead of me so when they make a decision they give me the order, and I come and implement the order ... If [I don't follow the order] then I'm the one going to face the punishment.'

'So your job is to punish any of these children, these boys who run away?' Ray continued.

'Yeah,' Anyang admitted, 'because the order given to me [was], "There's not any boy to leave the camp without any permission." So I give the order for them to be punished from morning until four.'

Ray appeared surprised by the answer. 'All day?' he asked, referring to the duration of the punishment.

'All day,' Anyang confirmed.

'Would they be tied up and stretched out?' Ray asked.

'Tied up and each of them have to receive fifty beat[s] of the cane,' Anyang explained. 'They set them down and then they have to be beaten. Fifty, each of them.'

Then the conversation turned to the real reason we were all there. 'So let's get into Ayik,' said Ray. 'Given what the punishment was, and he obviously kept running away, he was punished like this?'

'Yeah. I punished Ayik several times because he was still abusing the orders,' Anyang said. 'I was not targeting Ayik individually. That [punishment] belongs to everybody who is there. I have to give him the punishment.'

'Did you realise that tying someone to the ground with their legs up and their arms up was torture?' Ray probed.

'No,' said Anyang. 'By the time I was young I would think that I'm doing the right thing. I don't think about what they are feeling – pain or something like that.'

'You didn't think about that?' said Ray.

'No,' Anyang replied. 'I didn't think at the time, to be honest to you.'

'OK,' said Ray. 'You were just doing your job?'

'Yeah.'

'How do you feel about that now?' Ray asked.

'Regret,' Anyang offered.

'So you now agree that the punishment was cruel,' Ray proposed.

'That it was a mistake, yes,' Anyang replied.

'And it was torture?' Ray continued.

'Yeah,' Anyang agreed.

At this point Ray started to wind up the interview. 'In a few moments you'll meet Ayik,' he said. 'Do you understand what he must think of you?'

'I've got no idea, to be honest to you,' Anyang replied. 'I want to ask him for forgiveness. What I did to him, let's put it behind. Let us start a new relationship so we can build another life rather than going backwards. But now this will be his choice, but that's what I'm looking for.'

'When you look him in the eye, what will you be thinking?' Ray asked.

'I will be nervous seeing him, but I have to stand up,' said Anyang. 'For me to get the forgiveness from him I have to show something, that I'm really looking for the forgiveness. I will communicate with him through the eyes asking for the forgiveness.'

I was brought into the room and the lights were dimmed as Anyang and I looked into each other's eyes for five minutes. Anyang was dressed in a dark suit and wore black, wire-rimmed glasses that had a few chips of paint missing. They had seen better days and so too, it seemed, had Anyang.

As we stared at each other, those minutes felt more like hours. I couldn't really get a read on him. To me, his eyes were blank and I certainly couldn't see any regret or contrition written into his features. I hoped he was having better luck with me: I glared at him with a mix of emotions from rage, hatred and disgust to sorrow and pity. Although I was furious about the past, I knew Anyang had faced a lot of hardship, too. When the lights came back up he stood and hurried out of the room without saying a word.

'I didn't feel anything,' I told Ray in a debrief. 'It was just the face that he had in the army. That's all I see. I didn't feel that he's sorry. My mind was just looking and looking and his eye doesn't say anything.'

I was given some time to consider whether I wanted to go back and face Anyang and try to find resolution using words. In the end, I wanted to know what was inside Anyang's heart and I felt the best way was to ask him instead of looking him in the eyes.

'People can change,' I said to Ray. Hell, I should know – I wasn't the person I used to be. 'Maybe he *has* changed.'

When we re-entered and sat down, Anyang leaned towards me, extended his hands and spoke to me in Dinka. 'Ayik, Ayik. Greetings to you, brother. Greetings.'

I was stunned. I just sat there without acknowledging him, which made for an awkward TV stand-off. The confrontation was far more intense than I ever imagined it could possibly be. The moment I first saw Anyang at the wedding almost ten years earlier didn't really count as a confrontation; I had glared at him for less than a minute that day before taking off like a startled deer. The next time I saw him briefly at a party in Brisbane, the atmosphere was infused with alcohol and softened by my demeanour as a happy drunk. But this was real. There was no running away and no hiding inside a bottle.

'Greet me, Ayik,' Anyang pleaded in Dinka. 'Greetings. Greet me, please.'

Finally, I took his hands briefly and Anyang gently patted my shoulder. 'Sorry,' he said softly, before settling back in his seat. 'Sorry.'

The atmosphere was so strained that a falling pin would have sounded like a car crash. Rather than break the tension, the sound of Anyang's voice made it seem worse.

'Ayik,' he began, using English. 'I'm just asking you for the forgiveness. Please. I knew what I did was something wrong. It hurt you and you went through it all these years. I know it is still in your heart there but, please, I'm asking you, can you forgive me? Let us start a new chapter of life, please. Ayik, please.'

With that, the emotional dam inside me finally collapsed and tears poured down my cheeks.

'Please, Ayik, can you forgive me, please?' Anyang continued. 'Ayik, I beg you. Please!'

Anyang stood up from his chair, stepped towards me and tried to wipe the tears off my face. I pushed his hands away. 'Wipe! Wipe your face, my brother, please!' he implored me as he resumed his seat. 'Wipe your face,

I beg you, Ayik.' Anyang hung his head and looked at the floor, and we both sat there in the middle of the film set in silence.

Finally, I found my voice. 'Just . . . just going back to the training. You know, you put me in jail a few times.'

'Yes, yes,' Anyang agreed.

'There were a lot of other child soldiers there with me. I wanted to know exactly, did anybody . . . did you ever kill anyone in there? Whether this was a mistake, or what have you done? I wanted to know.'

'Actually, I didn't kill anyone there,' Anyang replied. 'See, to be honest to you, I knew what I did is something wrong. [A] mistake that happened – part of it because I was young and I was not well educated. Now I'm grown up so I know what is bad, what is good. I will prove it to you that I have changed. Let's work together, please. And I really appreciate it. I understand the feelings in your heart because every single night when the memories come up – what I did – it is there in my mind throughout. So when I revise what happened I don't feel comfortable when I don't sleep. I need a friend. I need a brother. I need someone so that we can share the ideas together. Where will I get that person? It is you, so please . . .'

I thought a moment then answered him. 'You know, the first time I saw you in church, my brain went blank because at first I didn't believe you were alive. I thought you were dead somewhere, and I used to pray to God that you'd get killed in the war [because] if you don't get killed and I get deployed with you, I'll kill you myself.

'I swear to God, Anyang,' I continued. 'There's no way you would have lived. I would have used everything. But it didn't happen and being here in Australia has taught me a lot of things: that I have life now, no one can control me. No one! No one can tell me what to do. No one can touch me – especially someone like you. No one hurt me like you did . . . you used to beat me up like a baby. I used to cry, Anyang. I used to run out of breath because I was crying and tied up – tied up in the sun just crying. I couldn't even stop [and] there was a point I can't cry any more – there was no tears. I can't even breathe properly, you know?

'Before I came here I went mental. If I'm mad, I used to break things. Everything – windows. And then, when I was here my life changed. I went for help but it took a long time to change because I had to learn again and try to live my childhood in the country because my childhood was taken away from me. I don't know if you understand, man. I don't know if you understand but losing my childhood, I'm living it through my child. I'm learning again to live for the things that I've missed. I play with him, I hold him and there's no one [who] hold[s] their kid like I do. I hold his hand, I bring him close.

'So I'm living through life right now – my childhood life and my adult life. And I don't want to live on like this now. I want to be able to, when I see you, say, "Hello!" Be happy, shake hands, you know? I want you to move on with your life. Any time you see me, don't think I have anything against you. It's like a scar – the scar is there, but I think it's healed now.

'I just want you to have the best in your life, man. Lucky that God help you by bringing you and me here. I want to live my life. I want to live happy. I don't want to think about this again. So you say you're sorry, yeah?'

'Yeah,' Anyang said.

'You're really sorry?' I pressed.

'Yeah.'

'I forgive you,' I said, 'and I mean it.'

When I said the words 'I forgive you', Anyang let out a deep sigh. It was a palpable release.

'I am finished with this today, here,' I continued. 'Just to move on and I wish you the best in everything you do. Go on with your life and be good, be good to everyone. But I have forgiven you.'

Anyang looked back at me and spoke in our ancient tribal language. 'Thank you, Ayik. Give me a hug. Stand up. Stand up, my brother Ayik. I'm sorry.'

I rose from my chair and embraced the man I had spent most of my life wanting to torture to death. The release was immense. As he clutched me close, Anyang again whispered closely into my ear, 'I'm sorry.' The words landed in my heart like the answer to a prayer and I wept with gratitude. At that moment – for the first time ever – I saw Anyang cry. It turned out both of us had some tears left to give.

'I'm going,' Anyang said, abruptly breaking from our embrace. 'I'm going, Ayik.'

And then, after all those years, he was gone.

EPILOGUE

From the day I filmed the TV segment with Anyang I was able to get on with my life with a degree of peace and acceptance for the first time. In forgiving my torturer I was also able to begin forgiving myself for the many terrible mistakes I have made and the people I have hurt since the war spat me out damaged and dangerous all those years ago.

Although I had never considered the wider implications of appearing on national TV, *Look Me in the Eye* exposed my vulnerabilities to hundreds of thousands of Australians and even to people in the UK, after Anyang and I were interviewed on BBC Radio. As a result, instead of persisting with the 'African way' and bottling my troubles up, I unwittingly chose to embrace the more open Aussie approach. These days in Australia it really is OK to talk about your problems. Doing so had a huge impact on me;

rather than wanting to kill Anyang, I stayed in touch with him and introduced him to my son instead.

I still have bad days sometimes – especially now that my son is around the age I was when I was carrying an AK-47 and surrounded by death. After all, it's normal and natural that some memories continue to resurface. In the wake of the SBS show, however, I received an outpouring of support and well wishes from all walks of life that have given me heart and strength. People I went to school with in Toowoomba came out of the woodwork to express shock and sadness about never knowing the suffering I endured in Africa. I can hardly blame them – after all, the only thing I told them for a long time was, 'Me Daniel. Me child soldier.'

Some people's reactions reduced me to tears. *It was great meeting you, Dan, my life would not have been the same without it*, a high school classmate named Craig wrote to me after the show had aired. *I hope you realise the hard work and effort you put into trying to fit in changed other people's outlook and set their foundation for how well they accepted other races.*

These sentiments only fired my resolve to be the best man I can be. The show also struck a powerful chord with a lot of the former child soldiers I'd gotten to know in Australia. Many of those guys have experienced similar problems to me, not least with PTSD and the attendant nightmare of self-medicating with drugs and alcohol. 'I'm so proud of you, man,' one ex-boy soldier told me. 'You've let people know about us and what we went through in the war. Some of us don't have the guts to talk about it because we're traumatised, but you have opened that door. Thank you.'

I was presented to my family's church in Toowoomba where the priest thanked me for helping the West understand what many South Sudanese and other African Australians had been through. 'You represent us all,' the priest said. 'By telling your story people will know that we Sudanese have a history of war and suffering. Hopefully this will help them understand why we're here.'

Sadly, the refusal of those who have suffered to share their problems and seek help can have terrible consequences. In 2002 I was informed that my buddy Daniel Deng Manyok took his own life while living somewhere in Kenya. The last time I saw Daniel was when I left the Ifo refugee camp in 1995 to get ready to come to Australia. I don't know why he killed himself but I can only imagine he was damaged by the war too. We'd been best friends but we had never once talked about the war. Now I wish we had. I have since become close with Daniel's family, particularly his sisters.

Following the death of my good friend Charles in Melbourne in 2003 I lost three more people close to me after they, too, moved to the southern capital. When I started pulling my life back together in the late 2000s, my ever-faithful friend Michael moved to Melbourne in search of a new start. He eventually died of liver failure in 2015. Another friend who shifted to the southern capital perished in a house fire, and yet another died after he was hit during a fight.

I count myself among the lucky survivors – not only did I make it through the war in Africa, I made it through my adjustment to the peace here in Australia. Somehow I dodged bullets, both real and metaphoric, on both continents. Importantly, I still have my whole family with me, too. I know there are African people out there today who are walking the planet completely alone. And then there are people like Anyang, whose family was obliterated. They may be living now in Canada, Australia, Europe or the United States without knowing where their loved ones are or what happened to them. When I think of them, I am reminded of the boy I saw drown in the river as I fled Ethiopia, never to be seen again. My heart breaks for all of them.

Sometimes, though, I get some news that makes my spirits soar. A few years ago one of my sisters went to Sydney to catch up with some people in the South Sudanese community there. A young guy somehow recognised her.

'Where is Ayik?' he wanted to know.

'Oh, my brother lives in Queensland,' she replied.

'Well, next time you see him, please thank him for saving my life,' he said.

He told my sister his name was Bul Aguang and that he had met me during the time I was stationed at Koi River. When my sister returned to Queensland she gave me his phone number and told me to call him. I thought it had to be a mistake or a prank. The last time I had seen Bul Aguang was at the camp in Kapoeta. I had assumed that he had been killed during the war.

A few days later I called the number.

'Bul Aguang, is that really you?' I asked.

'Heeey, Ayik!' he said. 'Yes, it's me, but you might not recognise me if you saw me because I have grown. If you see the scars on my neck, though, you'll know it's me.'

'Ohhh, that crazy fucking leopard!' I exclaimed.

We ended up laughing a lot as we had a good, long chat on the phone – I cried a bit, too. Bul Aguang had been in Kapoeta when it was overrun by Arab forces in 1992, not long after I was being bombed there.

'How the hell did you survive, man?' I asked Aguang. 'First the leopard then the Arabs?'

'I was lucky, Ayik,' he said. 'I was just plain lucky.'

'I know that feeling,' I told him as more tears welled in my eyes. 'I know luck only too well.'

It's been nearly thirty years since I last saw Bul Aguang face to face but I plan to visit him in Sydney and see the changes in him. And I really want to see those scars, too.

In 2018 I was lucky enough to reunite with another important person from my Red Army days. Former child soldiers came to Brisbane from all over the country to welcome this special person to Australia. Dozens of us gathered in Brisbane as a car was dispatched to collect the VIP from the airport. When the car pulled up at the house she was staying at later that afternoon, I was there to open the door for our guest of honour.

'Mamma Ring!' I beamed as she stepped out of the vehicle. It was the guardian nurse who used to treat the sick and injured Red Army boys in Dimma.

'Oh, you are one of my children from Dimma!' she said with a warm smile. 'There were boy soldier camps in other parts of Ethiopia but the ones who call me Mamma Ring are the boys from Dimma, where my own sons were trained.'

A few days later, Mamma Ring was honoured by a hall full of men she had cared for and comforted as terrified little boys. We laughed and cried and remembered those who weren't there, including her own two sons, who had been friends of mine.

Although it will always be a part of us, the Second Sudanese Civil War ended in 2005. After twenty-two years of fighting, it was one of the longest-running civil conflicts in history. Around two million people died, many of them civilians who succumbed to starvation and drought as the war tore the fabric of our society apart. A great many were wiped out in mass killings while another four million South Sudanese were displaced, including roughly half a million from the diaspora like me, who continue to reside in other countries.

In 2011, six years after a ceasefire agreement was struck in Nairobi, South Sudan gained its independence following a referendum in which 99 per cent of the population voted in favour of secession from the north. Today, the Republic of South Sudan remains the world's newest country and it has its capital in Juba, where I used to scavenge at the garbage dump as a boy.

Tragically, the great rebel leader Dr John Garang never lived to see his country born anew. He died in a plane crash in 2005, just days after he signed the peace agreement that eventually resulted in full independence. He was mourned by millions. My sister Aguil still keeps a framed photograph of him at her bedside. My son was born in 2006 and I named him after Dr John Garang. My son's mother and Aguil have always maintained a very good relationship, even when I was not around. Aguil and my son continue to have a strong bond.

My relationship with Aguil has been difficult at times, but when I reflect on all the people I need to apologise to and give thanks for, she is at the top of the list. Aguil fought so hard to pull our scattered family together during the war and bring us here safely to Australia. Indeed, hundreds of South Sudanese Australians owe her a debt of gratitude. She rescued many doomed people from the war. If it wasn't for Aguil I have no doubt whatsoever that I would have died in Sudan. I owe her my life, which means I owe my son's life to her as well.

The other guardian angel in my life, my brave and loving Aunty Dew, passed away in 2015 in Nairobi, Kenya. She not only saved me – as a proud rebel woman she also helped save South Sudan. I'm glad she lived to see her country liberated.

Although I am now sharing my story – warts and all – most of my family still refuse to speak about their experiences during the war, including my brother Deng, who fought with the rebels, too. I'm hardly one to judge, though – I shut my family out of my inner world for decades and it wasn't until *Look Me in the Eye* that any of them had a clue I was tortured as a child. Hopefully I can show them by example that a problem shared is a problem halved. Talking about my experiences is healing me. Every now and then there'll be tears or anger, but overall it's a blessing. I never thought I'd talk about my life and I was on track to take my terrible secrets to the grave. Now I think I will be able to die happy.

My ambitions for the rest of my life are simple. I want to be the best father and role model I can be, and I want to go as far as I can with my acting. Beyond that, my greatest goal has less to do with me than it does with my fellow human beings: I only wish to share my story in the hope it will help others overcome adversity. Hell, if someone as crazy as me can come through the fire and out the other side then there is hope for anyone.

ACKNOWLEDGEMENTS

Writing this book was emotionally much harder than I had ever anticipated, and yet it turned out to be a purifying and healing process. I have so much love for the following people – each of whom were a part of that journey with me – that I'm not quite sure where to begin.

The first time I ever saw a television was at a rebel army camp deep in the Ethiopian jungle. I was about twelve years old, and I'll never forget it was playing a movie called *Commando* starring Arnold Schwarzenegger. Arnie lived in a world of crazy rich white people, so different to mine that I never thought I might one day find myself transported there. How that happened is the story of this book.

After I arrived in Australia, journalist Ray Martin became a familiar face to me because he was so often on TV. Ray is one of the most respected and experienced journalists in Australia and in the world. He has done so much to make this a better nation, such as his work on *60 Minutes*. Ray had a similar hairstyle to Arnie's and I assumed he must be like all those Hollywood stars, with a fleet of limousines and surrounded by bodyguards. I couldn't have dreamed that our paths would ever cross. But from the first day I met him on the set of *Look Me in the Eye*, I felt a special connection. He quickly put me at ease before the cameras and he helped me through the difficult emotions and memories that show brought back for me. Since then, despite his many commitments, he has always been there for me when I have needed him, no matter how busy he is. Thank you, Ray. I am proud and honoured to call you a friend.

My thanks also to:

Debbie Cuell, executive producer for *Look Me in the Eye*. Without Debbie, my story would likely not have seen the full light of day.

Shine Endemol Australia and SBS Australia, for bringing *Look Me in the Eye* to life.

Meredith Curnow and Genevieve Buzo at Penguin Random House, for their unstinting support throughout the entire writing process and for giving me the opportunity to tell my story. Thanks also to publicist Alyssia El Gawly.

Craig Henderson, for his humour during long days of interviews and for helping me breathe life into the book. A true friend.

Nyibol Riek Makuei, the woman responsible for dressing me in African attire, which made me feel like a turtle when I landed in Australia.

Temucin Mustafa, for his close and loyal friendship with my family and me. Temucin started documenting my life in Australia via photography and video, and he encouraged me to follow my dreams of an acting career. He pointed me in the right direction and his interest in my welfare resulted in my graduation from acting school, my first speaking role in a TV series and the publication of this book.

Angus Murray of Irish Bentley Lawyers, for his support relating to the legal aspects of this book.

Journalist Richard Holdcroft, the first person to write about my childhood on news.com.au, and Karen Louise Jackman.

Thomas Harding Assinder, producer on *Outlook*, BBC World Service, for his interest in my story after *Look Me in the Eye* aired.

My counselling team, who helped me overcome my past: Dr Dilprasan De Silva (psychiatrist), Taher Forotan (counsellor/advocate) and my GP, Dr Ion Constantinescu.

Sergeant Robert Duffner, branch manager of the Fortitude Valley Police Citizen Youth Club (PCYC). Robert took me under his wing and gave me guidance and the ability to give back to the community. Thanks also to Sikeli Seru, administration officer at PCYC.

The St Vincent de Paul Society, for the help they have given me over the years.

Marcus Hogan and Sherri Smith from the Australian Performing Arts Conservatory, for guiding me through to graduation. I'd also like to give thanks to Ellen Leigh Birch for all her support during my acting classes and for being a longtime friend.

Gary Hopes, Bee Tran and Jaiden Kerp from Agency 888 Inc. Thanks also to Bud Hopes Casting, Manon Lewis and stunt actor/stunt rigger Peter Hill.

Film directors James McGrady (*Avengers: Endgame, Thor: Ragnarok*), Peter McLennan (*Don't Tell*), Glendyn Ivin (*Safe Harbour*) and Tom Michael McCaw (*Tidelands*) for providing me with great learning experiences on set.

A special thank you to John Riedel, for mentoring me through my high school years in Toowoomba. John stood right by me through the turbulent years that followed and remains a close and cherished family friend.

Daniel and Samantha Beasley, for being wonderful, supportive friends to my elderly mother.

David and Robyn Joy Wilkie, for their friendship and continued support.

Naseema Mustafa, for her kindness and caring.

I would like to acknowledge my lifelong best friends, Daniel Deng Manyok Deng Yak, Owar Obongo, Francis Athuai and Toby Daniel Juma Mingei.

To my friends Shaun Riggien, Vahidin Mujcic, Paul David Harrison, Craig Andrew McMahon, Kristen Armitage, Helen Maggs, Lisa Melinda Polley, the lovely Amanda Kannegiesser (the only friend who called me 'superstar'), Daniel Tuiara, Assad Elsair, Boris Jakopovic, Emily Darling and Cihan Mustafa – thank you.

My beloved family: my mother Achol Aguin Majok, my

late father Chut Deng Achouth, my late brother Aleer Chut Deng, my sisters Aguil Chut Deng, Yar Chut Deng and Akeer Chut Deng, brothers Deng Chut Deng and Garang Chut Deng, and my stepbrother Faris Chut Deng.

Thanks also to my nephews Dhieu Bair Mading and Dut Bair Mading, my nieces Agum Bair Mading and Aleer Aguil Chut, my aunty Adau Akoy Chol and my cousins Dew Manyok, Ruben Aguin Manyok, Ajak Manyok, Akuac Manyok, Akech Manyok, Akoi Manyok, and the late Majok Manyok. Thanks also to my cousin Gabriel Majur Akoi for his help with Dinka translation, and my sister-in-law, Efkedar Aklilu Werku.

Thanks also to the Right Reverend Bishop Daniel Deng Abot, Pastor Amos Lungile Maseva and Reverend Peter Deng Mayen.

While working on this book I was lucky enough to become a father for a second time. I would like to thank my baby girl, Achol Sunday Chut, and her mother, Tiva Lyn Cahill.

Finally, I owe a heartfelt and everlasting thank you to Mary, the lovely mother of my son. Our son.

Discover a
new favourite

Visit **penguin.com.au/readmore**